The Oryx Multicultural Folktale Series

Beauties and Beasts

The Oryx Multicultural Folktale Series

Beauties and Beasts

by
Betsy Hearne

Illustrated by
Joanne Caroselli

ORYX PRESS
1993

The rare Arabian Oryx is believed to have inspired the myth of the unicorn. This desert ante-lope became virtually extinct in the early 1960s. At that time several groups of international conservationists arranged to have 9 animals sent to the Phoenix Zoo to be the nucleus of a captive breeding herd. Today the Oryx population is nearly 800, and over 400 have been returned to reserves in the Middle East.

Copyright © 1993 by The Oryx Press
4041 North Central at Indian School Road
Phoenix, Arizona 85012-3397

Published simultaneously in Canada

Printed and Bound in the United States of America

∞ The paper used in this publication meets the minimum requirements of American National Standard for Information Science—Permanence of Paper for Printed Library Materials, ANSI Z39.48, 1984.

Library of Congress Cataloging-in-Publication Data
Beauties and beasts / [collected] by Betsy Hearne; illustrated by
    Joanne Caroselli.
        p. cm.—(The Oryx multicultural folktale series)
    Includes bibliographical references and index.
    Summary: Presents several versions of "Beauty and the Beast" and
"Cupid and Psyche," and provides several tales that reverse
traditional gender roles. Includes commentary on each tale,
activities, bibliographies, and a list of sources.
    ISBN 0-89774-729-1
    1. Cupid and Psyche (Tale)—Juvenile literature.   2. Beauty and
the beast (Tale)—Juvenile literature.   [1. Fairy tales.
2. Folklore.   3. Mythology.   4. Beauty and the beast (Tale)
5. Cupid and Psyche (Tale)]   I. Hearne, Betsy Gould.
II. Caroselli, Joanne, ill.   III. Series.
GR75.C8B43   1993
398.21—dc20   93-16
                                                 CIP
                                                 AC

In memory of John Donovan

Contents

Preface

The tales in this collection are as old as Rome and as new as you. They come from storytellers in Europe, Asia, Africa, the Middle East, and America. Beauty and the Beast have lived a long time, and they have a large family of related stories growing all over the world. The Beast takes many forms, usually animals common in the culture where the story originates—a lizard, for example, in the story from Indonesia, a dog in the variant from England, or a bull in the Scottish tale. Sometimes the Beast is simply a monster or a supernatural being disguised as—or thought to be—an animal. In every case, the Beast is transformed by the magic of human love. Beauty represents a spiritual hero or rescuer of the Beast more than she does the kind of physically attractive victim who is often called a "heroine." It is Beauty's courage, kindness, and perception that win happiness. Usually the Beast is a male who finds love in the form of a loyal young woman, but sometimes, as in "Kemp Owyne" and "Sir Gawain and the Loathly Lady," the Beast is a female transformed by the love of a goodhearted man.

Not all of the stories have the same plot or characters, but they all share similar motifs or basic story elements that form narrative patterns called tale types. To compare stories in a systematic way, folklorists have numbered the motifs and tale types that are common to many cultures. The number 425A has been assigned to the tale type of "The Monster or Animal as Bridegroom" (for example, "Cupid and Psyche") and 425C is the tale type number for "Beauty and the Beast," which is probably the most familiar to most readers and listeners. Tale type 425 represents the "Search for the Lost Husband," while tale types 400 ("The Quest for a Lost Bride") and 402A ("The Serpent Princess") include stories in which the male seeks and saves a monstrous or animalistic wife. Most of the stories here fall into the four tale types of 425, 425A, 425C, and 402A. They are related by common motifs and themes: a lonely beast; a loving human; and a family that threatens to separate the two until love can perceive, accept, and transform the strange beast to form a new family. Most of us will live through these symbolic patterns of experience, even if we don't number them by tale type. The stories survive because they describe such a common pattern in our own lives. We grow up and meet a stranger and begin to love him or her, but we must make a painful separation from childhood and family before we can be transformed into a loving partnership. Whatever names (or numbers) are assigned to Beauty and the Beast in these stories of transformation, the faces we see reflect our own.

Beauty and the Beast have lived both in and out of books. For this collection, I have selected some of my favorite versions from folklore and literature, two traditions that have influenced each other for centuries. The myth "Cupid and Psyche," for example, was written down by Aurelius around 150 A.D., but he probably heard it as a folktale from someone who couldn't read. Those who read his version told it to others who couldn't read, whereupon it re-entered the oral tradition and changed through the years until it was written down again and adapted into many different forms of literature. The oral and literary traditions have swapped stories back and forth, with movies and music introducing new elements. Although scholars don't always agree on what a folktale is, what it means, or where it comes from, storytellers have no trouble recognizing a good story and passing it on in whatever form they enjoy. This anthology is to enjoy and pass on.

The adaptations I've done have been minimal. It has always struck me that in tailoring folktales to a certain style for an anthology—the way Andrew Lang did, for example, in the *Blue Fairy Book* and others in his series—adapters risk losing the varied voices of the collected materials. Andrew Lang's stories are wonderful, but they all sound like Andrew Lang. Of course, when I *tell* a story, it does become my own, with newly imagined words and phrases; in that sense, every retelling is an original. But in assembling an anthology of this kind, which includes translations of famous literary tales, my goal has been to preserve as wide-ranging a diversity as possible. The book serves merely as a storage place; these tales won't really come alive until you tell them again in your own words.

Since "Beauty and the Beast" is a sophisticated fairy tale and "Cupid and Psyche" is a complex myth, the folklore related to these stories tends to be both sophisticated *and* complex. The audience for them is generally not the same as the audience for simpler folktales such as "The Wolf and the Seven Little Kids" or even "Cinderella." The stories here emphasize romance or courtship, subjects more of interest to older elementary, junior high, and high school students than to primary graders. However, this anthology would certainly serve as a resource for teachers and librarians working with younger children and adapting material for storytelling. It's important not to under-estimate what children, through a broad range of developmental stages, will find in any great story.

I have included "Beauty and the Beast," along with its variants, in the first section; even though it's not as old as "Cupid and Psyche," it's more familiar and less complex than the earlier tale, which dominates the second section. The last section, "Tales of Homely Women and Homemade Men," is devoted to stories that reverse traditional gender roles. Some of the women are beastly instead of beautiful; some wield powerful magic; some even create their own men, since they can't find any they like.

Each story is followed by a source note and brief commentary. For more background on "Beauty and the Beast," check the bibliography, which includes a book I have written on the history of the tale, *Beauty and the Beast: Visions and Revisions of an Old Tale*. You'll also find there some other folktale variants too numerous to fit into the anthology; a separate bibliography lists picture book versions and illustrated collections that allow artists to tell the story through graphic images. It's important, though, to keep descriptions and explanations in their place. Information may shed light on a story; and the suggested discussion or activities can enhance insights into a story, but nothing is more powerful than the experience of hearing a story.

Acknowledgments

Special thanks to Howard Batchelor, who invited me to be part of this series, who discussed it with me so intelligently, and who volunteered to do a new translation of "Cupid and Psyche" from the Latin and "Beauty and the Beast" from the French. Such editors should be listed as an endangered species. Thanks also to Joanna Hearne, who adapted "Sir Gawain and the Loathly Lady" from a medieval manuscript and who has developed, from long exposure, folklore-sensory perception. Sven Lohse enlisted Elena Tuskenis to translate "Eglė, Queen of Serpents" and told it in my course, "Story in the Oral Tradition," which has enriched me over the years as much as it has my students. Deborah Stevenson tracked down sources and citations with characteristic efficiency and quick-witted rejoinders. Roger Sutton read the manuscript and offered incisive criticism while refueling my sense of humor. And Elizabeth and Michael Claffey listened to the day-to-day stories, not all of them interesting.

Acknowledgments to Contributors

Katharine M. Briggs and Ruth L. Tongue. "The Small-Tooth Dog" from *Folktales of England* edited by Katharine M. Briggs and Ruth L. Tongue, copyright © 1965 by University of Chicago Press. Reprinted by permission of the University of Chicago Press.

Marie Campbell. "A Bunch of Laurel Blooms for a Present" from *Tales from the Cloud Walking Country* by Marie Campbell, copyright © 1958 by Indiana University Press. Reprinted by permission of Indiana University Press.

Richard Chase. "Whitebear Whittington" from *The Grandfather Tales* by Richard Chase, copyright © 1948, copyright renewed 1976 by Richard Chase. Reprinted by permission of Houghton Mifflin Company. All rights reserved.

Paul Delarue. "The Serpent and the Grape-grower's Daughter" from *French Fairy Tales*, selected and edited by Paul Delarue, translated by Austin E. Fife. Copyright © 1956, 1968 by Alfred A. Knopf, Inc. Reprinted by permission of Alfred A. Knopf, Inc.

Aurelio M. Espinosa. "The Enchanted Prince" from *The Folklore of Spain in the American Southwest* by Aurelio M. Espinosa, copyright © 1985 by the University of Oklahoma Press. Reprinted by permission of the Univeristy of Oklahoma Press.

Fanny Hagin Mayer. "The Monkey Son-in Law" from *Ancient Tales in Modern Japan: An Anthology of Japanese Folk Tales* selected and edited by Fanny Hagin Mayer, copyright © 1984 by Indiana University Press. Reprinted by permission of Indiana University Press.

Ruth Ann Musick. "The Dough Prince" from *Green Hills of Magic: West Virginia Folktales from Europe* by Ruth Ann Musick, copyright © 1970. Reprinted by permission of the publishers.

Dov Noy. "The Ten Serpents" from *Folktales of Israel* edited by Dov Noy, copyright © 1963 by University of Chicago Press. Reprinted by permission of University of Chicago Press.

Ronald W. Thomas and Rosemary Hyde Thomas. "Prince White Hog" reprinted from *It's Good to Tell You: French Folktales from Missouri* by Ronald W. and Rosemary Hyde Thomas, by permission of the University of Missouri Press. Copyright © 1981 by The Curators of the University of Missouri.

Barbara Walker. "The Princess and the Pig" from *A Treasury of Turkish Folktales* by Barbara Walker, copyright © 1988 by Linnet Books, Hamden, Connecticut. Reprinted by permission of the author and the publisher.

Rescued Beasts

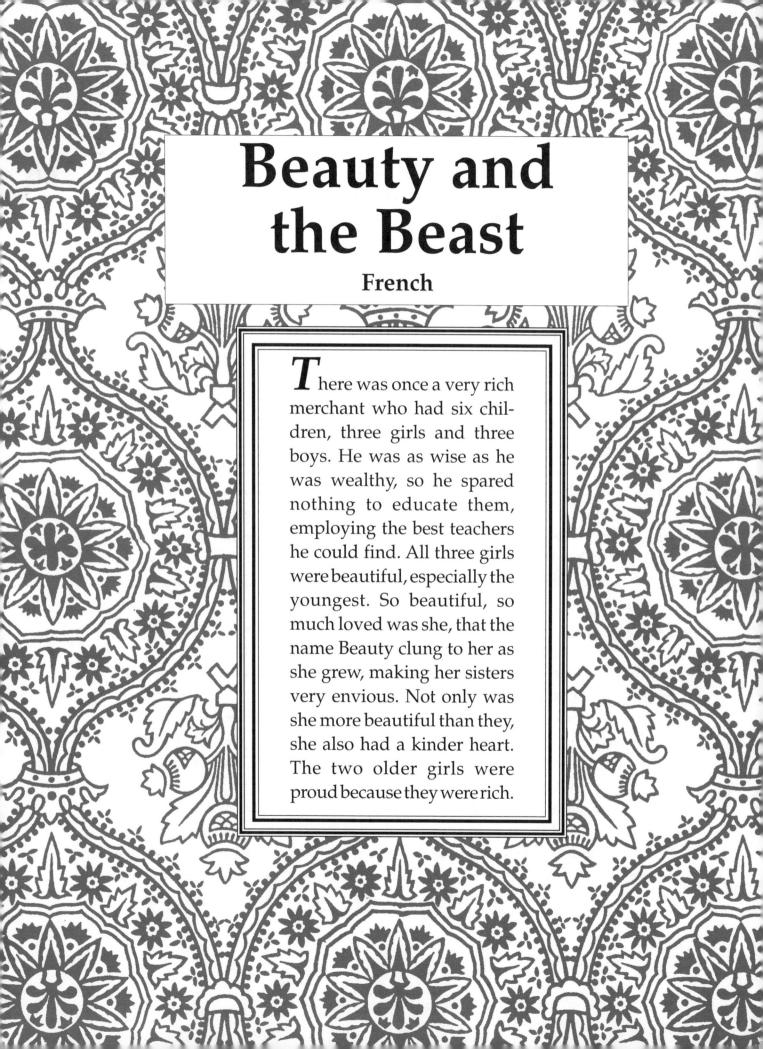

Beauty and the Beast

French

*T*here was once a very rich merchant who had six children, three girls and three boys. He was as wise as he was wealthy, so he spared nothing to educate them, employing the best teachers he could find. All three girls were beautiful, especially the youngest. So beautiful, so much loved was she, that the name Beauty clung to her as she grew, making her sisters very envious. Not only was she more beautiful than they, she also had a kinder heart. The two older girls were proud because they were rich.

Putting on airs like great ladies, they looked down their noses at the daughtersof other merchants; only aristocrats would do for them. Their days were idly spent in pleasure—at balls, the theater, or strolling in the park—and they mocked their younger sister, who spent most of her time reading good books. When it became known that the girls were rich, several well-to-do merchants made them offers of marriage, but the older girls' answers never varied: they would marry nobody of lesser rank than a duke, or at very least a count. Beauty had many suitors too, but she replied politely that she was too young to marry and preferred to spend several more years with her father.

But suddenly, the merchant lost his entire fortune; everything but a small country cottage far from the city. Weeping, he told his children that they would have to go and live there and that if they could bring themselves to work the land like peasants, they would be able to survive. The two older girls told him that would not be necessary: they had several lovers, any one of whom would be only too glad to marry, even though they no longer had fortunes. The good ladies could not have been more wrong. Their lovers would have nothing more to do with them now that they were poor. Their wealth had brought them attention, but no one loved them for themselves. In fact, there was rejoicing at their downfall, and some joked that their fine manners and haughty behavior would be very suitable for tending sheep. But for honest, gentle Beauty, who had always been kind to the poor, there was much sympathy, and several young gentlemen still wished to marry her, even though she hadn't a penny. To these she explained that she could hardly leave her father now that he needed her more than ever. She would follow him to the country to console him and help him work. Beauty was devastated at first by her loss, but at last she said to herself, "Crying did not bring me back my fortune; I must learn to be happy and poor."

When they arrived at their country house the merchant and his sons began to till the soil. Beauty rose at four o'clock in the morning and busied herself cleaning the house and making dinner for the family. At first she found this hard, for she was not accustomed to servant's work, but by the time two months had passed she had become stronger, and the heavy toil had given her perfect health. When her work was over she read, played the piano, or sang at her spinning wheel. Her two sisters, on the other hand, were bored to death. They rose at ten in the morning, strolled about all day, and amused themselves by lamenting over their lost pleasures. "See our young sister," they whispered to each other. "She has the soul of an animal, and she is so stupid that she delights in this unhappy situation." The good merchant, however, only loved his daughter more as her goodness and patience shone by comparison with her sisters' worthlessness. They, not content to leave her all the housework, insulted her whenever they could.

For a year or more the family lived in solitude when the merchant received news that a ship laden with merchandise belonging to him had arrived safely. The older girls were excited by this news and thought immediately of fleeing from the country. When they saw their father preparing to leave they begged him to bring them dresses, cloaks, hats, and all kinds of finery. Beauty asked for nothing, thinking that all the money her father might get for his merchandise would not be enough to buy her sisters what they wanted. "You've not asked me to buy you anything," her father said. "Because you are so kind as to think of me," said Beauty, "please bring me a rose, for we have none here." It was not that she really wanted a rose so badly but that she didn't wish to make her sisters seem greedy by asking for nothing herself.

The good man departed but found when he reached the market that he would have to go through a lengthy process to claim his possessions. After much trouble, he returned as empty-handed as he had left. With no more than thirty miles to go before he reached home, he found himself in a deep wood and became completely lost. It snowed heavily, and twice the wind threw him from his horse. Night fell and he began to think he would die of cold or hunger, or perhaps be eaten by the wolves he heard howling around him. But suddenly, at the end of a long wooded path, he saw a bright light at a great distance. Walking that way, he saw that the light came from a palace that was ablaze with light. Thanking God, the merchant hastened into the palace, but was astonished to find no one in the courtyards. His horse, who was following, found an open stable and immediately began to devour the hay and oats. The merchant tied him up and entered the house, where he found a great room with a fire roaring and a table set for dinner, but with no one in sight. The rain and snow had drenched him to the bone, but as he approached the fire to dry himself he nervously thought, "The master of this house, or his servants, will surely pardon my boldness when they arrive." He waited a long time, but when the clock struck eleven and no one had come he could no longer resist. Seizing a chicken, he ate it in two bites, trembling as he did so. He also drank several gulps of wine, which gave him courage to leave the main hall and cross several smaller private rooms, all magnificently furnished.

Eventually he found a bedroom. It was now well past midnight, and he was so exhausted that it took only a little more courage to close the door and go to bed.

At ten o'clock the next morning when he awoke he was astonished to see fine new clothes laid out in place of his own spoiled ones. "Certainly," he said to himself, "this palace must belong to some good fairy who has taken pity on me." Looking out the window, he saw that the snow had vanished and bowers of fragrant blooms delighted his view. He returned to the great hall where he had eaten the previous evening and found there a cup of chocolate on a small table. "Thank you, good fairy, for having the goodness to think of my breakfast." The good man drank the chocolate and went out to look for his horse. Passing a bower of roses he remembered Beauty's request and picked a branch so that she could have several. At that instant he heard a loud noise and there appeared a beast so horrible that he thought he would faint with fear.

"Ungrateful wretch," said the Beast in a terrible voice. "I have saved your life, welcomed you to my house, and now you repay me by stealing my roses, which I love more than anything in the world. You will pay for this with your death. You have only a quarter of an hour to beg God's forgiveness." The merchant fell to his knees and begged the Beast with clasped hands, "Forgive me Sir, I did not mean to offend you by picking a rose for one of my daughters." " Don't call me Sir, but Beast," replied the monster. "I despise compliments. Say what you think and do not try to touch my heart with flattery. You tell me that you have daughters. I will gladly pardon you on the condition that one of your daughters comes here voluntarily to die in your place. Don't try to reason with me. Go! Swear that if your daughters refuse to die for you, you will return in three months."

The good man had no intention of sacrificing one of his daughters to this evil monster, but he thought, "At least I shall be able to embrace them once more before I die." So he swore to return and the beast told him he could leave whenever he wished. "But," he added, "Don't go empty-handed. Return to the bedroom where you slept and you will find a large empty chest. Fill it with anything you want and carry it home with you." The Beast then vanished and the merchant said to himself, "If I must die, at least I won't have to leave my poor children destitute."

Beauty and the Beast

In the room where he had slept he found a large number of gold pieces. After filling the chest just as the Beast had told him, he closed it, found his horse, and left the palace weighed down by a sadness that equaled the joy he had felt when he entered it. His horse guided him down a woodland path, and before much time had passed he found himself at his own house once again. His children gathered round him, but instead of responding to their greetings he began to weep as he looked at them. He gave Beauty the branch of roses, saying, "Beauty, take these, they cost your father dearly." And quickly he recounted his dreadful adventure to his family.

The two older sisters screamed at Beauty when they heard this story, but she remained calm. "See what this little creature's pride has brought us," they said "A few small presents weren't enough for her—she wanted to be different. Now she has caused the death of our father, but it doesn't bother her at all." "What use are tears?" replied Beauty. "Why should I weep for my father's death? He isn't going to die. Since the monster will gladly accept one of his daughters, I will give myself up to his rage, and in dying I shall have the joy of saving my father and showing him that I love him." "No sister," said her brothers, "you shall not die. We shall find this monster and die by his blows if we cannot kill him."

"Give up that hope," their father warned. "This beast is so powerful that you would have no chance of killing him. I am touched by Beauty's kindness, but I have no intention of risking her life. I am old and have little time to live. What life remains to me will be well spent in defending yours." "I assure you father," said Beauty, "I will not let you return to that palace without me. Do not try to prevent me following you. Although I am young I am not so much in love with life, and I would rather be devoured by the Beast myself than endure the loss of my father." Having said this, Beauty insisted on leaving for the palace. Her sisters were delighted because her goodness had filled them with spiteful envy. The merchant was so overcome with sadness at the loss of his daughter that he quite forgot the chest that he had filled with gold, but as soon as he returned to his room to sleep he was astonished to find it at the foot of his bed. He resolved to say nothing of this wealth to his children because he knew they would wish to return to the city, whereas he was determined to die in the country. But he did confide the secret to Beauty, who then told him that several men had visited in his absence and two of them had proposed marriage to her sisters. She begged her father to let them marry. So kind was her heart that she bore them no grudge for the wrongs they had done to her.

The two evil sisters rubbed their eyes with onions to make them weep when Beauty left with her father, but her brothers were truly distraught. Only Beauty showed no signs of sorrow, not wishing to increase others' unhappiness. The horse took the road to the wood, and before nightfall they saw the lights of the palace, just as the merchant had before. The horse went alone to the stable and the good man and his daughter entered the great hall, where they found a lavish meal set for two people. The merchant had no heart for eating, but Beauty, forcing herself to remain calm, sat down and helped herself to food. "The Beast will want to fatten me before he eats me," she said to herself, "since he thinks of me as such a prize."

When supper was over they heard a great noise, and the merchant, knowing this was the Beast, tearfully said goodbye to his daughter. Beauty could not help trembling when she saw the Beast's horrible face, but she calmed herself as best she could. "Have you come of your own free will?" the monster asked. "Yes," she replied. "You are a good woman," said the Beast. "I am much obliged to you." Turning to the merchant he commanded him to leave in the morning and never return. "Good night, Beauty," said the Beast. "Goodnight, Beast," she replied. "Ah, daughter," said the merchant, embracing his child, "I am half dead with fear. Leave me here in your place." "No," said Beauty firmly. "You will depart tomorrow morning and leave me to God's help. Perhaps he will pity me." And so they retired, not thinking they would sleep, but their eyes closed as soon as they had lain down. In her sleep Beauty saw a vision of a lady who said, "The goodness of your heart, the bravery you have shown in giving your life to save your father's, gladdens me and will not go unrewarded." Beauty told this dream to her father when they woke, and although it comforted him a little it could not prevent him from weeping in desperation when the time came to leave his daughter.

As soon as he left, Beauty sat down in the great hall and began to cry herself, but since she was courageous she prayed to God and resolved not to pass the few remaining hours of her life in sadness. She firmly believed that the Beast meant to eat her that very evening. She decided to walk about the palace as she waited and was able, despite the circumstances, to admire its beauty. How surprised she was to find a door marked "Beauty's Apartment." Nervously she opened the door, and the magnificence of the place overcame her, but what surprised her most of all were the library, the piano, and several volumes of music. "He does not want me to be bored," she said to herself. But then she wondered. "If I shall live here for only one day, what need is there for all these arrangements?" This thought revived her courage. She opened the bookcase and saw a book on which these words were written in golden letters: "Wish, command, here you are queen and mistress." "Alas," she sighed, "I wish for nothing more than to see my father again, and to know what he is doing." She had said this to herself, so imagine her amazement when, glancing in a mirror, she saw there her house, where her father was arriving with a sad face. Then her sisters appeared before her, and despite the efforts they made to seem sorrowful, the joy they felt at losing their sister showed on their faces. All this disappeared a moment later, and Beauty could not help thinking that the Beast was kind and that she had nothing to fear from him.

At midday she found the table set and during her meal she heard an excellent concert, although no one was visible. In the evening, as she went to dinner, she heard the noise of the Beast and could not help trembling. "Beauty," said the monster, "do you mind if I watch you dine?" "You are the master," said Beauty trembling. "No," the Beast responded, "there is no master here but you. You have only to say 'Go' and I go. Tell me, don't you find me very ugly?"

"I do," said Beauty. "I cannot deny it. But I believe that you have a good heart." "You are right," said the Beast, "but apart from the knowledge that I am ugly, I have no understanding. I only know that I am a Beast." "There is no animal," Beauty replied, "that has such knowledge. The fool does not know he is foolish."

"Eat now, and amuse yourself in your house," the Beast urged her, "for everything here is yours and I shall be sad if you are not content." "You are full of kindness," said Beauty, "and when I think of your heart you no longer seem ugly." "Yes, my lady," he replied, "I have a good heart, but I am a monster nonetheless." "Many men are more monstrous than you," Beauty assured him, "and you please me, even with your ugly face, far more than those who hide a false, corrupt, ungrateful heart under a human smile." "If I had wit," said the Beast, "I would pay you a great compliment in thanks for your words, but I am a numbskull, and all that I can do is say that I am much obliged to you."

Beauty ate with good appetite. Her fear of the monster had almost vanished, but her heart recoiled when he asked, "Beauty, will you marry me?" It was several minutes before she responded. She feared to anger him, and she trembled when she said, "No, Beast." It seemed as though he wished to sigh, but could only gasp in a way so terrifying that the palace itself seemed to echo. Beauty was reassured, for the Beast sadly bade her goodbye, left the room, and returned from time to time to look at her again. Beauty, seeing his loneliness, pitied the poor creature. "Alas," she thought, "to be so ugly and yet so good!"

Three months passed happily enough. Every evening, the Beast would visit her and talk with good sense during supper, although he lacked what society would call wit or charm. Each day, Beauty discovered more signs of his goodness. She became accustomed to his ugliness and, far from fearing his approach, often looked at her clock to see if nine o'clock were near, for the Beast never failed to come at that hour. Only one thing distressed Beauty: The monster, before he left, would always ask her to be his wife and seemed overcome with sorrow when she refused. "You sadden me, Beast," she said to him one day. " I wish that I could marry you, but I am too honest to allow you to think that will ever happen. I will always be your friend; try to content yourself with that."

"It is just as well, " he replied, "that I know the truth. I am indeed repulsive, and yet I love you. I shall be content if you will remain with me. Promise that you will never leave." Beauty reddened at his words. She had seen in her magic mirror that her father was sick with grief and she wished to see him again. "I can promise that I shall never leave you altogether, but I have a longing to see my father, and I shall die of sadness if you refuse me this wish." "I would rather die myself than see you grieving," said the monster. "I will send you to your father, you will stay with him, and your poor Beast will perish." "Oh no," said Beauty. "I love you too much to cause your death. I promise to return in eight days. You have let me see that my sisters have married and my brothers have joined the army. My father is alone—let me stay with him for a week." "Tomorrow morning you shall be there," said the Beast, "but remember your promise. When you wish to return, you have only to leave your ring on the table as you sleep. Goodbye, Beauty." The Beast sighed as usual as he said these words, and Beauty went to bed sadly.

When she awoke in the morning she found herself at her father's house. The servant who appeared when she rang the bell beside her father's bed gave a cry of astonishment when she saw her. The good man came running when he heard the cry and might have died from sheer joy at the sight of his beloved daughter, whom he embraced for more than a quarter hour. When she had controlled her joy Beauty recalled that she had no fine clothes to appear in, but the servant told her that she had just discovered in the next room a great chest full of golden dresses decorated with diamonds. Beauty thanked the good Beast for his thoughtfulness, put on the least opulent of the dresses, and told the servant to lay out the others, which she intended to give to her sisters. But hardly had she given these instructions than the chest disappeared. Her father told her that the Beast wished these things to be kept for her and that the chest full of dresses would return to the same place.

As Beauty was dressing, the news of her return was brought to her sisters, who came running with their husbands. Both were most unhappy. The eldest had married a very handsome gentleman, but he was so enamored of his own good looks that he concerned himself with nothing else from morn 'til night, quite ignoring his wife's beauty. The other sister had married a most intelligent man who did nothing but aggravate people, his wife most of all. So the two were overcome with sadness when they saw Beauty dressed like a princess and more beautiful than the day itself. Her endearments only inflamed their jealousy, which increased still more when she told them how happy she was. So the two jealous sisters went out to the garden where they could not be overhead and poured out their spiteful, envious feelings. "Why is this creature happier than we are? Aren't we just as likeable as she is?" "Sister," said the elder one, "I have an idea. Let's try to keep her here more than eight days. This will goad the stupid Beast into a rage, and perhaps he will eat her." "You are right sister," said the other. "Let us show her how much we love her." And having made this resolution they returned and made such a show of affection to Beauty that she cried for joy. When eight days had passed the two sisters tore their hair, expressed great regret that they had to part and begged her to stay another eight days.

From this moment on Beauty reproached herself for the distress she was causing the Beast, whom she truly cared for. She missed his company. On the tenth night she had spent with her father she dreamed she was in the garden of the Beast's palace, and she saw him lying on the grass, cast down by her ingratitude. Beauty started out of her sleep in tears. "Am I not evil," she said to herself, "for making this Beast, who was full of kindness for me, so unhappy? Is it really his fault that he's ugly, and has so little intelligence? Why shouldn't I marry him? I shall be happier with him than my sisters are with their husbands! It is not a husband's looks or intelligence that make a wife happy; it is goodness of character, virtue, unselfishness, and the Beast has all these good qualities. I do not love him, but I respect and honor him as a friend. Come now! If I make him unhappy I shall regret it all my life." And with these words Beauty put her ring on the table and went to bed.

When she awoke she was overjoyed to find herself in the Beast's palace once again. She dressed herself with care to please him and waited impatiently all day for nine o'clock, but when the clock chimed the Beast did not appear. Beauty began to worry that her absence had killed him. Desperate, she ran about the palace calling for him, but having searched every room she remembered her dream and ran into the garden toward the canal, where in her vision he had been sleeping. She found him stretched out, seemingly lifeless, on the grass. Without fear of his face, she threw herself upon him, and, finding that his heart was still beating, she took water from the canal and threw it on his head. The Beast opened his eyes and said to Beauty, "You forgot your promise, and the pain of having lost you made me resolve to starve myself to death, but I shall die happy because I have the pleasure of seeing you again." "No, dear Beast," said Beauty, "you shall not die, but live to be my husband. I offer you my hand, swearing that I shall be yours always. Alas, I believed that I felt nothing but friendship for you, but the pain of separation made me realize that I cannot live without you." She had hardly spoken these words when she saw the palace ablaze with light, and fireworks and music seemed to proclaim a great festival, but her attention was fixed on her dear Beast, whose plight made her tremble. Imagine her surprise to discover that the Beast had vanished, and that before her stood a prince more beautiful than the God of Love, thanking her for ending his imprisonment by an evil spell. Although she was transfixed by this sight, she asked the prince what had become of the Beast. "You see him here before you," said the prince. "An evil witch condemned me to remain a Beast and hide my true nature until the day when a beautiful girl would agree to marry me. So you see there was no one but you in all the world who could perceive the goodness of my nature. I can offer you my crown, but I can never repay your kindness to me." Taking her hand, the Prince lifted her to her feet, and they went together into the palace, where Beauty was overjoyed to find her father and all her family, whom the good lady she had seen in her dream had transported thither. "Beauty," said this good lady (who was in truth a powerful fairy), "come and receive the reward of your good judgment. You preferred virtue over beauty and wit, so you deserve to find all these qualities united in one person. You will become a great queen, and I trust that this great honor will not destroy your goodness. As for you," and she turned to Beauty's sisters, "I see into your wicked hearts. You will become two statues, and your punishment will be that you will remain conscious beneath the stone. You will live at the doors of your sister's palace and your only suffering will be to witness her happiness every day. At the moment you recognize your own faults you can regain your human form, but I fear that you will always be statues. I can punish your pride, your anger, and your greed but to convert your wicked, envious hearts to goodness is a miracle that lies beyond my power." At this moment the fairy waved her wand and all that were in the room were transported to the Prince's realm where his subjects were overjoyed to see him. He married Beauty, and they reigned together in happiness for many years, for their perfect peace was built on virtue.

COMMENT: This is a translation of the French fairy tale that has most influenced "Beauty and the Beast" as we know it today in books and film. It was first published in 1756 by Madame Le Prince de Beaumont, a French aristocrat who included the story in a book called *Magasin des enfans* [sic], *ou dialogues entre une sage gouvernante et plusiers de ses élèves de la première distinction*, translated into English several years later as *The Young Misses Magazine, Containing Dialogues between a Governess and Several Young Ladies of Quality, Her Scholars*. Madame Le Prince de Beaumont intended "Beauty and the Beast" as a lesson for her students, so she shortened a 362-page version of "La Belle et la Bête" (1740) by Madame Gabrielle Susanne Barbot de Gallon de Villeneuve, who wrote fairy tale romances, drawn from earlier literature and folklore, for the entertainment of her friends at the royal court.

The Enchanted Tsarevitch

Russian

*O*nce upon a time there was a merchant who had three daughters. It so happened he had, one day, to go to strange countries to buy wares, and so he asked his daughters, "What shall I bring you from beyond the seas?"

The eldest asked for a new coat, and the next one also asked for a new coat; but the youngest one took a sheet of paper and sketched a flower on it. "Bring me, Papa, a flower like this!"

The merchant went and made a long journey to foreign kingdoms, but he never saw such a flower. So he came back home, and he saw on his way a splendid lofty palace with watchtowers, turrets, and a garden. He went for a walk in the garden, and you cannot imagine how many trees he saw and flowers, every flower fairer than the other flowers. And then he looked and he saw a single one like the one his daughter had sketched. "Oh," he said, "I will tear off and bring this to my beloved daughter; evidently there is nobody here to watch me." So he ran up and broke it off, and as soon as he had done it, in that very instant a boisterous wind arose, thunder sounded, and a fearful monster stood in front of him: a formless, winged snake with three heads.

"How dare you play the master in my garden!" cried the snake to the merchant. "Why have you broken off a blossom?"

The merchant was frightened and fell on his knees and besought pardon.

"Very well," said the snake, "I will forgive you, but on the condition that whoever meets you first when you reach home you must give me for all eternity. If you deceive me, do not forget, nobody can ever hide himself from me. I shall find you wherever you are."

The merchant agreed to the condition and came back home.

And the youngest daughter saw him from the window and ran out to meet him. Then the merchant hung his head, looked at his beloved daughter, and began to shed bitter tears.

"What is the matter with you? Why are you weeping, Papa?"

He gave her the blossom and told what had befallen him.

"Do not grieve, Papa," said the youngest daughter. "It is God's gift; perhaps I shall fare well. Take me to the snake."

So the father took her away, set her in the palace, bade farewell, and set out home.

Then the fair maiden, the daughter of the merchant, went in the different rooms and beheld everywhere gold and velvet. But no one was to be seen, not a single human soul.

Time went by and went by, and the fair damsel became hungry and thought, "Oh, if I could only have something to eat!" But before ever she had thought, in front of her stood a table, and on the table were dishes and drinks and refreshments; the only thing that was not there was birds' milk. Then she sat down at the table, drank and ate, got up, and it all vanished.

Darkness now came on, and the merchant's daughter went into the bedroom, wishing to lie down and sleep. Then a boisterous wind rustled round and the three-headed snake appeared in front of her.

"Hail, fair maiden! Put my bed outside this door!"

So the fair maiden put the bed outside the door and herself lay on the bedstead.

She awoke in the morning, and again in the entire house there was not a single soul to be seen. And it all went well with her; whatever she wished for appeared on the spot.

In the evening the snake flew to her and ordered, "Now, fair maiden, put my bed next to your bedstead."

She then laid it next to her bedstead, and the night went by, and the maiden awoke, and again there was not a soul in the palace.

And for the third time the snake came in the evening and said, "Now fair maiden, I am going to lie with you in the bedstead."

The merchant's daughter was fearfully afraid of lying on a single bed with such a formless monster. But she could not help herself, so she strengthened her heart and lay down with him.

In the morning the serpent said to her, "If you are now weary, fair maiden, go to your father and your sister. Spend a day with them, and in the evening come back to me. But see to it that you are not late. If you are one single minute late I shall die of grief."

"No, I shall not be late," said the maiden, the merchant's daughter, and she descended the steps. There was a carriage ready for her, and she sat down. That very instant she arrived at her father's courtyard.

Then the father saw, welcomed, and kissed her and asked, "How has God been dealing with you, my beloved daughter? Has it been well with you?"

"Very well, father!" And she started telling of all the wealth there was in the palace, how the snake loved her, how whatever she only thought of was in that instant fulfilled.

The sisters heard and did not know what to do out of sheer envy.

Now the day was ebbing away, and the fair maiden made ready to go back and was bidding farewell to her father and her sisters saying, "This is the time I must go back. I was bidden keep to my term."

But the envious sisters rubbed onions on their eyes and made as though they were weeping. "Do not go away, sister. Stay until tomorrow."

She was very sorry for her sisters and stayed one day more.

In the morning she bade farewell to them all and went to the palace. When she arrived it was as empty as before. She went into the garden and saw the serpent lying dead in the pond! He had thrown himself out of sheer grief into the water.

"Oh my God, what have I done!" cried out the fair maiden. She wept bitter tears, ran up to the pond, hauled the snake out of the water, embraced one head, and kissed it with all her might. And the snake trembled and in a minute turned into a good youth.

"I thank you, fair maiden," he said. "You have saved me from the greatest misfortune. I am no snake, but an enchanted Prince."

Then they went back to the merchant's house, were betrothed, lived long, and lived for good and happy things.

COMMENT: "The Enchanted Tsarevitch" is drawn from the folktale collections published by Aleksandr Nikolaevich Afanas'ev between 1855 and 1864. In the Russian variant, the father promises to give the Beast whatever he meets upon arriving home, a motif that often appears in this tale type; the German variant here, "The Singing, Soaring Lark," and the Appalachian "Whitebear Whittington" both contain the same incident. Notice, too, how the nineteenth-century Russian story has repeated a detail from the eighteenth-century French, the sisters' rubbing their eyes with an onion to simulate grief. Russian fairy tales contain many enchantments, both of men freed by women, as in "The Enchanted Tsarevitch," and of women freed by men, as in "The Snake Princess" and "Maria Morevna."

The Princess and the Pig

Turkish

*O*nce there was and once there wasn't a padishah [king] who had three daughters, each one more beautiful than the one before. One morning as he set off for town the padishah asked, "What shall I get for you at the market?"

His oldest daughter said, "Please bring me a golden gown, Father."

His second daughter said, "Please bring me a silver sash, Father."

The youngest daughter said nothing at all.

"Well, daughter?" asked the padishah, smiling at her, for she was his favorite.

"Nothing at all, Father," she answered.

"Come, now, my daughter. Ask for whatever you want most."

"Well, then, Father, you may bring me

Grapes that speak,

Apples that smile,

And apricots that tinkle in the breeze.

Her father smiled, but the older girls laughed aloud. Their sister *was* an odd one.

As for the padishah, he climbed into his carriage and drove off to the market. He found the golden gown and the silver sash easily enough. He found grapes a plenty, but none that spoke. He found apples in heaps, but none that smiled. He found apricots by the dozens, but none that tinkled in the breeze.

He looked through the market again and again, and still he could not find what his youngest daughter wanted. At last he climbed into his carriage and set off for home.

While he rode, he thought about his daughters. As for the horses, they took the short way to the palace. Suddenly the carriage stopped.

The padishah looked up in surprise. There was the carriage, mired in the mud. The Padishah touched the horses' backs with the whip. They pulled and pulled, but they could not move the carriage at all.

The padishah sent his footman to get more horses, but even pulling all together, they could not move the carriage out of the mud.

"*Now* what am I to do?" sighed the padishah.

Suddenly, "*Grmph, grmph, grmph,*" there was an ugly old pig rooting through the mud. The padishah pulled his arms back inside the carriage. Ugh! What a filthy creature!

"*Grmph, grmph, grmph,*" said the pig. "I can push you out of the mud."

"Well, then," said the padishah, "*push.*"

"*Grmph, grmph, grmph,*" grunted the pig. "First you must promise to give me your youngest daughter as my bride."

The padishah swallowed hard. Give his favorite daughter to a pig? Never! On the other hand, he could not just stay there in the mud . . .

"Very well," he said. "You may have my youngest daughter. Quickly, now! Push my carriage out of the mud."

"*Grmph, grmph, grmph!*" grunted the pig. And with one push of his snout, the carriage was out of the mud and onto the road. Off drove the padishah, without even a thank-you for the pig, ugly old thing that he was.

The oldest daughter was glad for her golden gown. The second daughter swished here and there in her silver sash. And the youngest was so sweet tempered that she didn't mind the least bit that her father hadn't brought her

> *Grapes that speak,*
> *Apples that smile,*
> *And apricots that tinkle in the breeze.*

As for his promise to the pig, the padishah never said a word about it. After all, what use would a pig have for a princess!

Still, later that afternoon there was a "*Grmph, grmph, grmph,*" in the palace courtyard. The padishah rushed to the door, and, sure enough, there was that ugly old pig, hauling a wheelbarrow. "*Grmph, grmph, grmph.* I have come for your daughter," said the pig.

"Oh, dear!" thought the padishah. And he called a maid from the kitchen. She was quickly dressed in a fine silk gown, with slippers to match. "Here you are," said the Padishah as he set the girl carefully in the wheelbarrow.

"*Grmph, grmph, grmph,*" grunted the pig crossly, and he tipped the girl out of the wheelbarrow into the dust. "I came for your youngest daughter," said he, "and it is your youngest daughter that I want."

Well, there was nothing to do but to tell his youngest daughter all about it. Nonetheless, he had her dressed in a ragged gown, with torn slippers. Perhaps the pig would not want her after all.

But the pig knew a beautiful, sweet-tempered girl when he saw one. "*Grmph, grmph, grmph,*" he grunted happily. "Yes, this is the one I want." And he tucked her into the wheelbarrow and trundled her off down the road.

"There goes my daughter," sighed the padishah. "And all for being stuck fast in the mud!"

The pig and the princess went along and went along and went along till they came to a tumbledown old pigsty. "*Grmph, grmph, grmph.* Here is your new home," said the pig, and he helped her down from the wheelbarrow. Into the pigsty they went.

"*Grmph, grmph, grmph,*" said the pig pointing with his trotter to the trough. "You'll find corn a plenty to eat. And over there"—he pointed to straw littering one corner—"that is your bed."

Now the princess was a good-tempered girl, and this wasn't exactly what she was used to. Still, she munched away at the corn, and early in the evening she curled herself up to sleep in the straw. But once the pig was snoring away, the princess wept salt tears for sorrow. At last, she too fell asleep.

The sun was high in the sky by the time she awoke. And what was this! She found herself lying in a feather bed, with sheets of softest silk. The bedroom in which she lay was finer than her own room in the palace. And everywhere there were maids to wait upon her.

She rubbed her eyes in astonishment, and when she looked again, there stood a smiling young man, handsome as the full moon. "You see, my dear," said he, "this is my palace, and you are my queen. As soon as I came to the throne, a wicked enchantment was worked upon me, and I was turned into an ugly pig. Only one thing would release me from the spell. I had to win a girl who asked for

Grapes that speak,
Apples that smile,
And apricots that tinkle in the breeze.

"Come, now, to the garden and see for yourself." And he led her down a winding staircase to the garden.

"Good morning, my queen," said the grapes, thick upon the vine. Apples smiled at her from every bough. And, true enough, golden apricots tinkled as the breeze touched them.

The princess sighed happily. "Let us go this very day and tell my father," she said.

The young king and the princess went in a fine coach to the padishah's palace. He was overjoyed to hear the news. A splendid wedding was celebrated for forty days and forty nights. As for the young king and his bride, they had all their wishes fulfilled. May we have a share of their good fortune!

COMMENT: As in most Beauty and Beast stories, it is the daughters' requests that start the action of this Turkish version, in which the youngest shows her true heart by asking for something natural—fruit here, flowers in other versions—instead of demanding superficial, materialistic decoration to beautify herself. Ironically, the natural proves magical in leading to a transformation of two lives, the heroine's and the rescued hero's.

A Bunch of Laurel Blooms for a Present

Appalachian

*B*rought you some laurel buds to make a flowerpot to pretty up your house. Mary always loved laurel blooms the best when they were still little, knobby, pink buds, kinda square shaped. Giving you a bunch of laurel blooms puts me in mind of an older tale about a girl that wanted laurel blooms for a present.

It starts with a man going off from home a far piece to tend to some business, and he asked his three girls what they wanted him to bring them back for presents. The oldest girl said she wanted him to bring her back a green silk dress. The middle girl said she wanted him to bring her a pair of gold beads. The youngest girl wanted him to bring her a bunch of laurel blooms for a present. Maybe they had moved down to the level country from the mountains, and she was used to seeing laurel blooms back where they used to live. I don't know. The tale don't say.

The man bought the green silk dress and the pair of gold beads as soon as he got to the far-off place. But he waited about the laurel blooms till he was ready to start back home, so they wouldn't get all wilted. Then he couldn't find any laurel blooms. He looked and he looked. After a time he saw some laurel blooms on the edge of a wood. Seemed like they didn't belong to nobody, so he picked some to give his youngest girl for a present.

After he picked the laurel blooms, an old witch came out of the laurel bushes and said they belonged to her, and she didn't aim to let nobody pick them. She said he had already picked some, and he would have to die. He told her the flower blooms were a present for his youngest girl. Then the old witch said he could live if he would give his youngest girl to her.

He would rather die than do that. He begged the old witch to let him go home and give the presents to his girls. She said he could do that. He gave the green silk dress to the oldest girl and the pair of gold beads to the middle girl. They put on their finery and primped in front of the looking glass. He gave the laurel blooms to the youngest girl, and she hugged his neck and kissed him. Then she put her present of flower blooms in a flowerpot of water to keep them fresh. Her sisters made fun of her for asking for nothing but flower blooms when she coulda had fine things to wear.

The man told his girls he had to go live with the witch, and the youngest girl ran off in the night and went in his place to save him from the old witch. The old witch put her to live in a nice little house with an upstairs. A good supper was fixed and on the table waiting. The youngest girl saw two places at the table. Then in came the biggest toad-frog she ever did see.

It sat down in one chair, and she sat down in the other chair, and they ate supper together. The toad-frog washed up the dishes and told her to rest from the long journey. She went upstairs and found a room with a nice bed and lay down to sleep. In the night she could see by the candle the big toad-frog climbing into her bed. She went back to sleep, and in the morning when she woke up, he was gone. He had breakfast ready when she went downstairs, and all the time he cooked and kept house. He treated her kind and good, but she couldn't like his warty old skin and his toad-frog eyes. Living with a man-size toad-frog would give a girl the creeps, it seems to me. But she learned to love his kind and helpsome ways, though not his looks.

He picked laurel blooms every day and brought them to her for a present. She felt like she could live out her days with him, if only he looked like a natural human. One night she woke up thinking about it. In the moonlight she could see a handsome young man lying in the bed beside her and the warty old frog skin hanging on a bed post.

She eased out of bed, got the warty old frog skin in her hands, and tiptoed down-stairs. She flung the warty old frog skin into the fireplace and watched it crackle and burn. Then she went back to bed and slept sound till morning.

It was a handsome young man woke her up next morning. He told her he could stay a man now. Burning up the warty old frog skin had lifted the witch's spell on him. They lived there amongst the laurel blooms together in the nice little house with an upstairs.

Her sisters were jealous all their lives for her having such a handsome man that would cook the breakfast and give her a house with an upstairs. Maybe they learned their lesson about being greedy and wanting costly presents and ending up with not so much as the youngest sister that asked for nothing more than a bunch of laurel blooms.

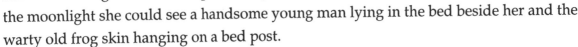

COMMENT: In this down-home Appalachian version, the heroine's burning the ugly toad skin that disguises her handsome husband proves enough to break the spell. In other versions (such as "The Three Daughters of King O'Hara") the heroine loses her husband if she or her relatives try to destroy his disguise, and she suffers for such impatience by having to search for him long and hard.

The Small-Tooth Dog

English

*O*nce upon a time, there was a merchant who traveled about the world a great deal. On one of his journeys thieves attacked him, and they would have taken both his life and his money if a large dog had not come to his rescue and driven the thieves away. When the dog had driven the thieves away he took the merchant to his house, which was a very handsome one, and he dressed his wounds and nursed him until he was well.

As soon as he was able to travel the merchant began his journey home, but before starting he told the dog how grateful he was for his kindness and asked him what reward he could return. The merchant said he would not refuse to give the dog the most precious thing that he had.

And so the merchant said to the dog, "Will you accept a fish that I have that can speak twelve languages?"

"No," said the dog, "I will not."

"Or a goose that lays golden eggs?"

"No," said the dog, "I will not."

"Or a mirror in which you can see what anybody is thinking about?"

"No," said the dog, "I will not."

"Then what will you have?" said the merchant.

"I will have none of such presents," said the dog, "but let me fetch your daughter and take her to my house."

When the merchant heard this he was grieved, but what he had promised had to be done, so he said to the dog, "You can come and fetch my daughter after I have been at home for a week."

So at the end of the week the dog came to the merchant's house to fetch his daughter, but when he got there he stayed outside the door and would not go in. But the merchant's daughter did as her father told her and came out of the house dressed for a journey and ready to go with the dog.

When the dog saw her he looked pleased and said, "Jump on my back, and I will take you away to my house." So she mounted on the dog's back, and away they went at a great pace until they reached the dog's house, which was many miles off.

But after she had been a month at the dog's house she began to mope and cry.

"What are you crying for?" said the dog.

"Because I want to go back to my father," she said.

The dog said, "If you will promise me that you will not stay at home more than three days I will take you there. But first of all," said he, "what do you call me?"

"A great, foul, small-tooth dog," said she.

"Then," said he, "I will not let you go."

But she cried so pitifully that he promised again to take her home. "But before we start," said he, "tell me what you call me."

"Oh!" said she. "Your name is Sweet-as-a-honeycomb."

"Jump on my back," said he, "and I'll take you home." So he trotted away with her on his back for forty miles, when they came to a stile.

"And what do you call me?" said he, before they got over the stile.

Thinking that she was safe on her way, the girl said, "A great, foul, small-tooth dog." But when she said this, he did not jump over the stile, but turned right round about at once and galloped back to his own house with the girl on his back.

Another week went by, and again the girl wept so bitterly that the dog promised to take her to her father's house. So the girl got on the dog's back again, and they reached the first stile as before. Then the dog stopped and said, "And what do you call me?"

"Sweet-as-a-honeycomb," she replied.

So the dog leaped over the stile, and they went on for twenty miles until they came to another stile.

"And what do you call me?" said the dog, with a wag of his tail.

She was thinking more of her own father and her own home than of the dog, so she answered, "A great, foul, small-tooth dog."

Then the dog was in a great rage, and he turned right round about and galloped back to his own house as before. After she had cried for another week, the dog promised again to take her back to her father's house. So she mounted upon his back once more, and when they got to the first stile, the dog said, "And what do you call me?"

"Sweet-as-a-honeycomb," she said.

So the dog jumped over the stile, and away they went—for now the girl made up her mind to say the most loving things she could think of—until they reached her father's house.

When they got to the door of the merchant's house, the dog asked, "And what do you call me?"

Just at that moment the girl forgot the loving things that she meant to say, and began, "A great, . . . " but the dog began to turn. She got fast hold of the doorlatch and was going to say "foul," when she saw how grieved the dog looked and remembered how good and patient he had been with her, so she said, "Sweet-as-a-honeycomb."

When she had said this she thought the dog would have been content and galloped away, but instead of that he suddenly stood up on his hindlegs, and with his forelegs he pulled off his dog's head and tossed it high in the air. His hairy coat dropped off, and there stood the handsomest young man in the world, with the finest and smallest teeth you ever saw.

Of course they were married and lived together happily.

COMMENT: In her book *Folktales of England*, Katharine Briggs introduces "The Small-Tooth Dog" as a nineteenth-century folktale collected by Sidney O. Addy and later published in his *Household Tales with Other Traditional Remains, Collected in the Counties of York, Lincoln, Derby, and Nottingham* (London, 1895). There's also a lively Appalachian variant called "The Girl That Married a Flop-Eared Hound-Dog" in Marie Campbell's book *Tales from the Cloud Walking Country*.

The Small-Tooth Dog

The Fairy Serpent

Chinese

*O*nce there was a man who had three daughters, of whom he was devotedly fond. They were skillful in embroidery, and every day on his way home from work he gathered some flowers for them to use as patterns. One day when he found no flowers along his route homeward he went into the woods to look for wild blossoms, and he unwittingly invaded the domain of a fairy serpent that coiled around him, held him tightly, and railed at him for having entered his garden.

The man excused himself, saying that he came merely to get a few flowers for his daughters, who would be sorely disappointed were he to go home without his usual gift to them. The snake asked him the number, the names, and the ages of his daughters and then refused to let him go unless he promised one of them in marriage to him. The poor man tried every argument he could think of to induce the snake to release him upon easier terms, but the reptile would accept no other ransom. At last the father, dreading greater evil for his daughters should they be deprived of his protection, gave the required promise and went home. He could eat no supper, however, for he knew the power of fairies to afflict those who offend them, and he was full of anxiety concerning the misfortunes that would overwhelm his whole family should the contract be disregarded.

Some days passed; his daughters carefully prepared his meals and affectionately besought him to eat, but he would not come to the table. He was always plunged in sorrowful meditation. They conferred among themselves as to the cause of his uncommon behavior, and, having decided that one of them must have displeased him, they agreed to try to find out which one it might be by going separately to urge him to eat. The eldest went, expressed her distress at his loss of appetite, and urged him to partake of food. He replied that he would do so if she would for his sake marry the snake to whom he had promised a wife. She bluntly refused to carry out her father's contract and left him in deeper trouble than before.

The second daughter then went to beg him to take food, received the same reply, and likewise declined to fulfill the engagement he had made. The youngest daughter then went and entreated him to eat, heard his story, and at once declared that if he would care for his own health properly, she would become the bride of the serpent. The father therefore took his meals again, the days sped without bringing calamity, and the welfare of the family for a time seemed secure.

But one morning as the girls were sitting at their embroidery, a wasp flew into the room and sang:

Buzz! I buzz and come the faster;
Who will wed the snake, my master?

Whenever the wasp alighted the girls prodded him with their needles and followed him up so closely that he had to flee for his life. The next morning two wasps came, singing the same refrain; the third morning three wasps came; and the number of wasps increased day by day, until the girls could no longer put them to rout, nor endure their stings.

Then the youngest said that in order to relieve the family of the buzzing plague, she would go to her uncanny bridegroom. The wasps accompanied her on the road and guided her into the woods where the fairy serpent awaited her in a palace that he had built for her reception. There were spacious rooms with carved furniture inlaid with precious stones, chests full of silken fabrics, caskets of jade, and jewels of gold. The snake had beautiful eyes and a musical voice, but his skin was warty and the girl shuddered at the thought of daily seeing him about.

After the wedding supper, at which the two sat alone, the girl told her spouse that she appreciated the excellence of all that he had provided for her and that she should perform all her domestic duties exactly. For many days she kept the house neat, cooked the food, and made all things pleasant for her repulsive bridegroom. He doted upon her and pined whenever she was out of his sight. So heedful was he of her wishes and her welfare that she grew to like his companionship and to feel a great lonesomeness whenever he was absent.

Having no help in her household work, she was, one day, on finding the well dried up, obliged to go into the forest in search of water, which she finally discovered and toilsomely brought back from a distant spring. On returning she found the snake dying of thirst, and in her eagerness to save his life she grasped and plunged him into the water, from which he rose transformed, a strong and handsome man. He had been the subject of wicked enchantment, from which her dutiful quest and gracious pity set him free. Thereafter she often with her admirable husband visited her old home and carried gifts to those who were less happy than she.

COMMENT: *A Type Index of Chinese Folktales* by Nai-Tung Ting lists many variants of "The Snake Husband" (Tale Type 433D, which combines the opening of 425C and parts of 408), along with this variant of Beauty and the Beast, which appeared in A. M. Fielde's *Chinese Fairy Tales*, published in 1893. Enchanted men also turn up in Chinese folklore as frogs, and beautiful maidens as plants!

Monkey Son-in-Law

Japanese

*O*nce upon a time there was a farmer. The sun shone day after day one year and his family's rice fields dried up. No more water came, and the soil cracked. The farmer sat on the border of his paddy and said to himself, "If only somebody would come and water my field that can grow 1000 bundles of rice, I would give him whichever of my three daughters he wanted."

Just then a monkey came rustling out of the bamboo grass thicket and said, "If I put water on your paddies, will you give me one of your daughters?"

"Of course I will," declared the farmer. Then the monkey went far above on the hill and lots of water came down to the paddies that could produce 1000 bundles of rice. They filled to the brim before the farmer's eyes. He was delighted. "Day after tomorrow is a good day," he said, "so come then to get my daughter."

The farmer worried that when he went home his daughters would refuse. That night he would not eat his supper before he went to bed. His oldest daughter went to him and asked, "Why don't you eat? Hurry and get up." He said, "I am worried about something. Will you do something for me?"

The girl answered that she would do anything her father said, but when her father said he wanted to send her to the monkey as a bride she got angry. She said, "Was there ever such a fool as Father! Who wants to go to a monkey's place!" She stamped on her father's head as she went off.

Then the second girl came, and when she heard what he had to say, she kicked his pillow and ran away. His third daughter came and said, "Get up quickly, Father. Supper is ready."

When her father told her what was on his mind, she said, "I will go to the monkey's place as a bride if Father tells me to, or even to a snake. I'll do anything you say, so hurry and get up."

That made the old man happy. He got up and ate his supper.

On the proper day the monkey appeared in a red sleeveless coat to get his bride. The old man took out the good clothes his wife had worn when she was young and dressed up his daughter. He gave her to the monkey, who led her far back in the hills. There they lived together on good terms.

Presently spring came again. The girl said to the monkey, "I want to go home for a visit. Please make Father's favorite burdock leaf mochi [sweet rice cake] and carry it for me." The monkey agreed and set about making it while she prepared to go. He steamed the rice and made burdock leaf mochi. He was going to put it into the lunch box, but the girl said, "If you put that into the lunch box it will smell of the box and Father won't eat it."

The monkey asked if he should put it in the kettle, but the girl said it would smell of the kettle and her father would not eat it. The monkey said, "I will leave it in the mortar [a heavy bowl for pounding food] and carry it on my back." The two started off together, the monkey trudging along with the mortar on his back.

Along their way was a river where beautiful cherry blossoms bloomed on its banks. The girl asked the monkey to pick some of the blossoms to make her father happy. The monkey agreed and started to set the mortar down to get ready to climb a tree. The girl said, "If you put the mortar down, the mochi will smell of dirt and it won't be fit to eat."

So the monkey climbed with the mortar on his back. He tried to break off a branch that was right and asked the girl, but she told him to climb a little farther. He asked, "How about here?" She told him to go farther.

Finally, when she said it was just right, the branch broke off and the monkey fell into the river with the mortar on his back. As he was carried away by the current, he called:

My life washed away in Sarusawa without a regret;
Later the girl will surely weep.

The girl did not cry at all. She hurried back to her home where her father wept for joy. Her older sisters laughed at her because she returned from the monkey's home. They turned into rats for being disloyal to their father and scurried off into the rafters of the house.

COMMENT: Although it begins like a traditional Beauty and Beast tale, this Japanese variant is the only story in the collection that doesn't end with a transformation, and it's included as a contrast to our expectations: here's a heroine who decides to go back home and live happily ever after with her father. Whether the heroine can be said to take control of her fate or simply continues subservience to her father is open to question. Although some Beauty and Beast tales—the Lithuanian story, "Eglė, Queen of Snakes" and the French tale, "The Ram," for example—end tragically when the Beauty forsakes the Beast or their children betray him, this unusual Japanese variant turns into a trickster tale.

The Lizard Husband

Indonesian

*O*nce there was an old woman who lived alone in the jungle and had a lizard she brought up as her child. When he was full grown, he said to her, "Grandmother, go to the house of Lise, where there are seven sisters, and ask for the eldest of these for me as a wife." The old woman did as the lizard requested and, taking the bridal gifts with her, went off; but when she came near the house, Lise saw her and said, "Look, there comes Lizard's grandmother with a bridal present. Who would want to marry a lizard! Not I."

The old woman arrived at the foot of the ladder, ascended it, and sat down in Lise's house, whereupon the eldest sister gave her betel [the leaves and nut of a plant], and when her mouth was red from chewing it, asked, "What have you come for, Grandmother? Why do you come to us?" "Well, Granddaughter, I have come for this: to present a bridal gift. Perhaps it will be accepted, perhaps not. That is what I have come to see."

As soon as she had spoken, the eldest indicated her refusal by getting up and giving the old woman a blow that knocked her across to the door, following this with another that rolled her down the ladder. The old woman picked herself up and went home.

When she had reached her house, the lizard inquired, "How did your visit succeed?" She replied, "O! Alas! I was afraid and almost killed. The gift was not accepted; the eldest would not accept it. It seems she has no use for you because you are only a lizard."

"Do not be disturbed," said he. "Go tomorrow and ask for the second sister." The old woman did not refuse, but went the following morning, only to be denied as before. Each day she went again to another of the sisters until the turn of the youngest came. This time the girl did not listen to what Lise said and did not strike the old woman or drive her away, but agreed to become Lizard's wife, at which the old woman was delighted and said that after seven nights she and her son would come.

When this time had passed, the grandmother arrived, carrying the lizard in a basket. Kapapitoe (the youngest sister) laid down a mat for the old woman to sit on while she spread out the wedding gifts. The young bride gave her food, and after she had eaten and gone home, the lizard remained as Kapapitoe's husband. The other sisters took pains to show their disgust. When they returned home at night, they would wipe the mud off their feet on Lizard's back and say, "Pitoe can't prepare any garden; she must stay and take care of her lizard." But Kapapitoe would say, "Keep quiet. I shall take him down to the river and wash off the mud."

After a while the older sisters got ready to make a clearing for a garden, and one day, when they had gone to work, the lizard said to his wife, "We have too much to bear.

Your sisters tease us too much. Come, let us go and make a garden. Carry me in a basket on your back, wife, and gather also seven empty coconut shells." His wife agreed, put her husband in a basket, and, after collecting the seven shells, went to the place they were to make ready for their garden. Then the lizard said, "Put me down on the ground, wife, so that I can run about." He scurried around, lashing the grass and trees with his tail and covering a whole mountainside in the course of the day. With one blow he felled a tree, cut it up by means of the sharp points on his skin, set the pieces afire, and burned the whole area, making the clearing smooth and good.

Then he said to Kapapitoe, "Make a little seat for me, so that I can go and sit on it." When this was done, he ordered the seven coconut shells to build a house for him, after which he was carried home by his wife. The older sisters, returning at evening, saw the new clearing and wondered at it, perceiving that it was ready for planting. When they got home they said to their sister, "You can't go thus to the planting feast of Ta Datoe. Your husband is only a lizard." Again they wiped their feet on him.

The next day Lizard and his wife went once more to their clearing and saw that the house had already been built for them by the coconut shells, which had turned into slaves, whereupon Lizard said, "Good, tomorrow evening we will hold the preliminary planting festival, and the next day a planting feast." Ordering his seven slaves to prepare much food for the occasion, he said to his wife, "Let us go to the river and get ready." But on arriving at the stream, they bathed far apart, and the lizard, taking off his animal disguise, became a very handsome man dressed in magnificent garments.

When he came for his wife, she at first did not recognize him, but at last was convinced. After she had been given costly new clothes and ornaments, they returned toward Lise's house. As they came back, the preliminary planting festival had begun, and many people were gathered, including Kapapitoe's elder sisters, Lise, and the old woman. The six sisters said, "Tell us, Grandmother, who is that coming? She looks so handsome, and her sarong rustles as if rain were falling. The hem of her sarong goes up and down every moment as it touches her ankles." The old woman replied, "That is your youngest sister, and there comes her husband also." Overcome with jealousy, the six sisters ran to meet their handsome brother-in-law and vied with each other for the privilege of carrying his betel-sack, saying, "I want to hold the sack of my brother-in-law." He, however, went and sat down, and the six went to sit beside him to take him away from their youngest sister, but the lizard would have none of them.

Next day was the planting, and his sisters-in-law would not let the lizard go in company with his wife, but took possession of him and made him angry. Accordingly, when Lise and the sisters were asleep, the lizard got up, waked Kapapitoe, and taking a stone, laid four pieces of bark upon it and repeated a charm, "If there is power in the wish of the six sisters who wipe their feet on me, then I shall, when I open my eyes, be sitting on the ground just as I am now. But if my wish has power, when I open my eyes, I shall be sitting in my house and looking down on all other houses." When he opened his eyes, he was seated in his house high up on the mountain, for the stone had grown into a great rock, and his house was on top of it. His sisters-in-law tried to climb the cliff, but in vain, and so had to give up, while he and his wife, Kapapitoe, lived happily ever after.

COMMENT: More than any other Beauty and Beast variant, this Indonesian tale, published in a volume called *Oceanic Mythology* (1916), contrasts the kindhearted youngest child (in a family of seven girls) with her arrogant sisters, who wipe the mud off their feet on the lizard's back. It is the youngest girl's acceptance of the lizard as husband that initiates his emergence into manhood, though the actual transformation seems to happen independently as he bathes in the stream near his wife. Water often figures in these transformations, as in the case of the Fairy Serpent's transforming drink of water, or even the canal water with which Beaumont's Beauty tries to revive her Beast.

Questing Beauties

Cupid and Psyche

Greco-Roman

*O*nce, hundreds of years ago, in a city of ancient Greece, there lived a king and queen who had three beautiful daughters. The two older daughters were very good-looking, though not so beautiful that their good looks cannot be described, but the youngest daughter's beauty was so dazzling that words cannot even begin to express it. Struck dumb with wonder, the crowds of people who came from far off to see this famous sight could only kiss the fingertips of their right hands at the sight of her as if they were worshiping Venus, the goddess of beauty herself. So the rumor soon spread among nearby cities, and even in foreign countries, that the goddess who had been born—so the legend said—from the blue of the sea and the white spray of the waves had now taken the form of a mortal woman; or, in another story, that the earth had given birth to a rival goddess, younger and more pure than the first.

Day by day these stories spread throughout the islands and mainland of Greece and even to the shores of Italy and Africa, and great crowds of people traveled by land and sea to see this marvelous sight. No one sailed anymore to Cyprus, or even to Cythera, where the main temple of Venus stood empty, its floors unswept and its altars covered in dirty ashes. It was the young woman Psyche whom people worshiped now. Whenever she appeared people would strew her paths with flowers and garlands, invoking the name of Venus with feasts and holidays and striving to honor the goddess, whose power they still feared.

This extravagant attention paid to a mere girl sent the real Venus into a violent and uncontrollable rage. She knew very well that her earthly rival was mortal, but she was jealous even so, and her wounded pride made her spiteful: "Am I to endure the humiliation of neglect while my place is taken by an imposter? Shall I allow my heavenly name to be profaned by association with this common woman? Did it mean nothing that the shepherd Paris, in the world's first beauty contest, chose me as the most beautiful of the goddesses? This woman, whoever she is, shall soon wish that she was not born beautiful."

So right away she sent for her notorious son, Cupid, that destructive boy with wings who roams about at night breaking into people's houses armed with flames and arrows, breaking up good marriages, spreading shameful mischief, and doing absolutely nobody any good. This boy was naturally wild, but what Venus did now egged him on to even worse nastiness. She took him to the city where the beautiful Psyche lived and told him the whole story of her rival's attractions.

"I beg you for the love you have for me, by the delicious wounds of your arrows, by the sweet burning of your flames, revenge your mother and punish that woman. Do this for me and I will forgive you everything you have done or ever will do. May that girl fall passionately in love with the lowest, meanest, filthiest and most despicable creature in the whole world."

And so saying she kissed her son and walked straight into the sea—or over it rather, because the water and all the gods, great and small, that inhabit it began at once to do what she wished, as if she had given her orders in advance. By the time she reached the open sea a small army of minor gods and goddesses escorted her in a chariot drawn by Tritons, one of whom shielded her from the sun with a shade while another held up a mirror so that she could admire herself as she splashed along.

But if she could have looked into Psyche's heart she would have realized there was no need to revenge herself on a helpless girl. Poor Psyche was already miserable. She took no pleasure in her beauty. Although people came from far and wide to worship her, none was so brave as to ask to marry her, and although she was admired constantly she might just as well have been a statue or a painting in a museum. Her two older sisters, who were beautiful in just a common, everyday sort of way, had long ago accepted marriage offers from local royalty, but Psyche stayed home without a lover or even a friend. She was sick in mind and body and began to hate that beauty that everyone else found so pleasing.

Psyche's father, thinking he might have done something to offend the gods, made a long journey to the famous oracle of Apollo at Miletus. There, after praying and sacrificing, he asked the god to bring his daughter a husband. The god replied, but not as the man hoped. Instead he gave these strange and menacing instructions: "Dress her for her wedding, but prepare her for her funeral, and lay her on a mountain top. There expect her to meet, not a bridegroom, but a winged and snake-like monster so horrible that Jove himself and all the gods, the rivers, and even Hell itself, shall be afraid."

The once-happy king returned sadly home and told his wife what the oracle had said. They wept for several days, but could not delay what had been prophesied. When they lit the wedding torch it burned black and smoky; the cheerful music of the flute and the marriage hymn turned to a mournful wail; the bride wiped away tears with her wedding veil. The whole city closed and all business was suspended as the people joined in the grief of their king and queen.

At last brave Psyche was led from her house in a great procession that should have been joyous but instead was filled with mourners. Her parents, struggling to resist what cruel fate had decreed, tried to walk slowly, but Psyche herself, realizing that her own beauty had condemned her, urged them to do as the oracle had commanded: "Envy is to blame for this. When people came to bring me praise and worship my beauty, calling me Venus, and giving me honors that were due to the goddess—that is when you should have grieved! Take me to the mountain. I am eager to see this husband of mine. Why should I try to put off the coming of the creature that will end the world?"

Having said this Psyche fell silent and rejoined the procession slowly climbing the mountain. When they came to very top they abandoned her, left the bridal torches, extinguished by their tears, and sadly made their way home. Her unhappy parents shut themselves up in their house and resolved never to see daylight again.

Meanwhile Psyche, trembling and crying, was sitting at the edge of the cliff when Zephyr, the soft wind, gently blew into the folds of her dress and with a gentle breath lifted her from the mountain and carried her tenderly to the flowery grass in the valley far below. Calmed by her flight to this soft bed, with fears and anguish vanished, she fell into a peaceful sleep.

She awoke to find herself in a grove of tall trees beside a spring of clear water. Nearby stood a great palace that she knew immediately was not the work of human hands, but the home of a god. So luxurious was this building, and so crammed with every possible sign of art and wealth, that Psyche's curiosity overcame her fear and she wandered about the splendid rooms, marveling at what she saw and wondering why these treasures were unlocked and unguarded. And as she gazed in wonder she heard a voice that seemed to come from nowhere: "My lady, don't be astonished at all this wealth. It is yours! Go to your bedroom, sleep, and take a bath. When you are refreshed your servants will bring you a feast fit for a king."

As if in a trance she obeyed the voice, first sleeping and then washing away her weariness. No sooner had she sat at a table when unseen hands brought her a banquet. It was as if the wind had brought her wine and food, and then there was music, but no musicians. At last, when the evening star appeared, she went to bed, but she was wakened in the middle of the night by a gentle bell-like sound. Now more than ever she was afraid what might become of her in this strange place. As she lay there fearfully a man came silently to the bed, made love to her, but then left before dawn as silently as he had come. At dawn invisible servants came to care for her, as was the custom in those times after the first night of the honeymoon. Strange though all this was to Psyche, she was not alarmed. A mysterious voice kept her company in her loneliness, and many days and nights passed just like her first.

Meanwhile Psyche's parents grew old and worn down by constant grief, and the story of her terrifying end spread as quickly as the fame of her beauty. Soon her sisters heard of it and deserted their own homes to compete with one another in showing sympathy for their parents.

That night Psyche's mysterious and invisible husband spoke to her for the first time: "Dearest Psyche, darling wife, a great danger threatens you. Your sisters are distraught with the news that you are dead and will soon come to the top of the mountain looking for some trace of you. If you should hear their weeping, pay no attention. Do not even look that way. If you do, you will cause me great pain, and completely destroy yourself."

She humbly promised to obey, but as soon as he had left, the sense of her isolation crept over her. Deprived of human friendship and unable to see her own sisters, she felt trapped in a prison of meaningless wealth and luxury. Refusing to eat, she went to bed early that night, and her husband came to her early and began to scold her: "Is this how you keep your promise, Psyche? What can I expect of you if you never stop tormenting yourself? Very well, follow your heart, but remember my warning before it is too late."

Then she pleaded with him and threatened to die of unhappiness if he did not allow her to see her sisters and speak to them. So at last he gave in, even allowing her to give her sisters whatever presents of jewels and gold she wished. But he warned her sternly not to listen to their advice that she find out what her husband looks like. If she did try, he warned, she would never feel his arms around her again.

Psyche was comforted by this and even felt bold enough to wheedle one more concession from her husband. "I would rather die a hundred times than lose your caresses! I love you, whoever you are, more than my own life. I would not compare Cupid, the god of love himself, with you. So please do one more thing for me. Ask your servant Zephyr the wind to carry my sisters here the same way he brought me." And wrapping herself around him she murmured endearments in his ear such as "sweetheart," "my dear husband," and other nonsense until he gave in and promised he would do everything she wanted. When daylight came he once again vanished.

Meanwhile, Psyche's sisters found the cliff where she had been abandoned and set up an enormous commotion of wailing and sobbing so that the rocks themselves began to shake at the noise. Hearing the sound of her name Psyche came running from the palace and commanded Zephyr to bring her sisters gently down to the valley, where the three had a tearful but ecstatic reunion.

Then Psyche, eager to share her good fortune, invited her sisters into the palace and displayed all its luxuries, including the servants who were never visible. Very soon all this wealth and beauty replaced the guests' pleasure with envy, and one of them began to question Psyche. "Who owns all these treasures?" "What kind of man is your husband?" But Psyche did not forget her husband's warning, and she made up a story that he was a handsome young man with barely a shadow of a beard who spent most of his time hunting in the fields and mountains. Afraid that she might betray the truth if she went on talking, she loaded her sisters with jewels and summoned Zephyr to take them back to the mountaintop.

No sooner had they returned home than the sisters dropped their pretense and began to complain long and loudly to one another about their bad luck. "What right has she to all those things?" they grumbled. "Why, she doesn't even know how to appreciate them." And on and on they went, pouring scorn on their own husbands and sneering at Psyche's pretensions, although, as we have seen, she had put on no airs and only wished to share her pleasure with her sisters. Possessed by envy, the evil pair plotted to conceal all that they had learned and hatched a scheme to return another day to Psyche's palace and take revenge. They hid the precious gifts that Psyche had given them, carried on their fake grief, and went back to their homes to plot.

But Psyche's husband, who seemed to know exactly what was in their minds, did all he could to warn Psyche about the danger she was in. "Those evil wretches are plotting against you. They will try to persuade you to sneak a look at my face." He told her exactly how they would try to excite her curiosity and advised her to hear and say nothing when they raised the subject. And then he told her a dangerous and awesome secret: Psyche was pregnant. If she kept her husband's trust, the child would be an immortal god; but if she tried to betray him, the child would be a mere human and marked for death like all of its kind.

Psyche was filled with joy at this news, thought proudly of her motherhood, and anxiously counted the days of her pregnancy, unaware that as the child grew bigger inside her, so did her sisters' desire for revenge. Her husband, who clearly saw the danger, warned her once again, "If you value our happiness, do not see those women again. Do not listen when they call from the cliff, making the rocks shake with their false cries of grief." But just as before, Psyche protested that she would never reveal his secret, asked for his trust, and persuaded him to let her see her sisters again. "If I cannot see your face surely you will let me see theirs?"

This time the sisters did not even stop to see their parents but rushed straight from their ships to the cliff and threw themselves off. That would have been the end of the story if faithful Zephyr had not been waiting to do his master's bidding. He caught them in midair and delivered them gently to the ground. Concealing their hatred with bland smiles, the sisters greeted Psyche and congratulated her on her state, which was by now obvious to anyone. "Oh, our little baby is going to have a baby of her own! What luck for the family, and what fun we will have! If he looks anything like his parents he will be a real Cupid of a boy."

Just as before, Psyche made her sisters welcome and treated them to all the pleasures that her palace could provide until, at last, seated round the dinner table, the conversation turned back to Psyche's husband. "What kind of man was he exactly, and what was his family like?" Psyche, simple and goodhearted woman that she was, completely forgot her earlier story about the young hunter and described her husband as a middle-aged merchant from the neighboring region who was rarely home because he traveled so much about his business. Nervously she stuffed her sisters' clothing with gifts and once again sent them on their way.

Zephyr had hardly raised them in the air when they began: "So, the young man with the soft beard is now a distinguished businessman. Obviously she is either telling lies or she really doesn't know what he looks like. Either way we must part this fool from her wealth. If she doesn't know what he looks like then she must have married a god and that baby she is carrying will be a god too. If she becomes famous as a mortal who gave birth to a divine child I shall kill myself."

They slept little that night and barely spoke to their parents. The next morning found them back at the cliff again. Hardly stopping to bring out some fake tears they bore down on Psyche with their own story. Just as the oracle had predicted, Psyche's mysterious husband was a loathsome snake. The villagers hereabouts had seen it swimming in the stream. When Psyche's pregnancy was near its end, this creature would eat her and the child. Now that she knew the worst, they said, the decision was up to her. Would she take the advice of her loving sisters and flee, or would she prefer to go on sleeping with a snake?

Terrified, the simple and guileless girl forgot her husband's warnings and confessed that she did not know what he looked like. She told them that he was always threatening her with dreadful punishments if she looked and begged them to help her. Now that she was defenseless in their hands they told her what they really wanted her to do. "No danger will prevent us from trying to save our own dear sister. We have this scheme planned down to the last detail. Listen carefully. Hide a very sharp knife and a lamp near your bed. When you hear your husband's breaths coming deeply and slowly light the lamp and cut off the snake's head with your right hand. As soon as he is safely dead, we will come to rescue you and find you a decent man for a husband."

Having done this mischief the evil sisters, afraid to be around while their plot was carried out, lost no time in returning to their ships by the usual route, leaving Psyche alone with her thoughts. Nothing she had suffered in the past had prepared her for these torments. She knew she had to do what her sisters demanded; she knew she must discover the identity of the creature she called her husband. Was he really a snake? She hated the idea of a snake, but in her heart she still loved her husband, whatever he might be. So as night began to draw near she quickly hid a lamp and a knife. Her husband came, and after making love to her he fell asleep.

Now Psyche, given strength and resolution by a fate she could not avoid, lit the lamp and grasped the knife, ready to kill what she loved. But as the light fell on the bed she saw that she was lying beside the wildest and most beautiful creature of all: Cupid, the god of love himself, lay there sleeping. Psyche was completely overcome by the sight, and in her weakened state would have killed herself with the knife, except that the sharp blade, as if with a life of its own, slipped harmlessly to the floor.

Gazing at her husband, and revived by the power of her love for him, she began to recover her strength. She saw his white skin and rosy cheeks, his golden hair that fell in ringlets, competing with the lamp in brightness, and on his shoulders the soft white feathers of his resting wings, along whose edges the tiny white plumes continued to shiver. No hair disfigured his perfect body, so anyone would have known that this was the son of Venus without needing to see the weapons of Cupid, the bow and arrows that lay at the foot of the bed. As Psyche studied the sleeping god she could not resist reaching out and taking one of the arrows from the quiver and testing its point with her thumb. Her hand trembled, she pushed too hard, and there on her skin a drop of red blood appeared. And so, by her own hand, and completely unaware of what she was doing, Psyche fell in love with love itself. Overcome by passion she leaned over her husband, covering him with kisses, and yet afraid to wake him from his deep sleep. At this moment the lamp—whether she knocked it or whether it, too, longed to touch the god's body—sputtered hot oil onto Cupid's shoulder. In an instant he woke and fled without a word.

But not before Psyche managed to grab his right leg with both hands so that she trailed after him sadly as his wings took him into the clouds. At last she fell to the ground and Cupid, instead of simply flying away, returned and spoke to her, for he, too, was deeply upset. "Poor foolish Psyche. For you I disobeyed the orders of my mother, who told me to chain you to some ugly creature in marriage. Instead I made you my own lover. But that, as I now realize, was a foolish thing to do. I shot myself with one of my own arrows and enslaved myself to someone who took me for a wild beast and was planning to cut off my head. You see now why I warned you against your sisters. I shall take my revenge on them, but I will punish you now just by leaving."

With these bitter words he flew away, leaving Psyche to gaze hopelessly after him as long as he remained in sight. Then, when he vanished, she threw herself into a nearby river, intending to end her sorrow once and for all. But the river, afraid, perhaps, of what Cupid might do to him, lifted her up and gently laid her on a grassy bank where, quite by chance, the god Pan, ruler of the woods and fields, happened to be flirting with the mountain goddess, Echo. Pan was teaching her songs that she sung back to him. He had an idea of what had happened to Psyche and so, in his rough but kindly way, he called her to him and tried to comfort her. "Pretty lady," he said, "I am just a rough countryman, a shepherd by trade, but I am old and experience has taught me things. I would guess from the way you look that you are in love. Don't try to kill yourself again. Stop grieving and pray to Cupid. Try and win his help by devotion, for he loves pleasure and has a heart that is easily won."

Psyche said nothing, but bowed respectfully to Pan and set out as fast as she could to the home of one of her sisters. There she related exactly what had happened, but when she came to the end of the story, she changed one detail. She told her sister that as Cupid left he had said he was going to punish Psyche by marrying her sister instead. Hearing this the sister immediately told her husband some lie about going to visit her parents, jumped on a ship, and traveled once again to the cliff overlooking Cupid's place. There she cried out "Take me Cupid, take me!" and leaped into the air. But no Zephyr was there to help her this time. Her body shattered on the rocks and the corpse made a fine meal for the buzzards and rats. Without pausing to find out what had become of her, Psyche traveled to the home of her other sister, where she told exactly the same story, with the same result.

As Psyche roamed about in search of Cupid, the god lay in his mother's bedroom, groaning from the pain of his wound. A cackling seagull who had seen him there dived into the ocean to find Venus and tell her the whole story. "Not only that," added the gossiping bird, "but the business of beauty and love is getting a bad reputation. People are saying that you and Cupid have left your duties and that there is no joy, no charm, and nothing is done gracefully. Civilization is dying, and marriage is going out of style."

Venus flew into one of her vile tempers and commanded the bird to tell her the name of her son's girlfriend, expecting that it would be a Nymph, a Muse, or at very least one of the Graces that wait on her. "Oh no," said the tattling bird. "It's a girl, and her name is Psyche." "What," said the goddess, "that tart who wanted to borrow my name? Did he think I wanted to introduce him?" And off she flew to her bedroom, where she found Cupid just as the bird had said. Then Venus made a very long, angry, and rather coarse speech containing references to Cupid's private life, and even to her own relationship with Mars, the god of war, who was not Cupid's father. Finally, she threatened to put Cupid under the power of her own greatest enemy, Sobriety, a filthy old hag whom they both feared more than anything.

As she stormed off she met Juno and Ceres, who asked why she was in such a rage. She told them her disgrace and asked their help in finding Psyche, but they put on their most reasonable manner and pointed out that Cupid was not as young as he looked and had every right to choose his own wife. They pointed out that she, in her younger days, had not been above doing the same. "How can you sow the seeds of desire in the world while in your own house you forbid love affairs." The truth was that both Juno and Ceres were quite afraid of Cupid's bow and did all they could to please him, but their defense only made Venus angrier and she hurried on toward the sea.

Still Psyche continued to look for Cupid, believing that if she could not soften his anger with her love, she could still try to appeal to him with prayers. So she sought out first the temple of Ceres, goddess of the harvest who feeds the world, and then the temple of Juno, protector of married women, but neither would help her for they owed a loyalty to Venus and dared not risk angering her. Feeling that she had no other hope and could not long escape the revenge of Cupid's mother, Psyche decided to go directly to the house of Venus and throw herself on the mercy of the goddess. "Besides," she thought, "perhaps I shall find him there too, right in his mother's house." And so she began to consider what she would say.

By now Venus had grown tired of looking for Psyche on earth and called for her chariot—the one that Vulcan, the god of fire, had made for her when they were married. On sea, Venus was transported by dolphins and other sea creatures, but in the air she

Cupid and Psyche

was drawn along by birds—this time four white doves. The heavens opened for her and she headed straight for the throne of Jupiter to ask his permission to use the help of Mercury, the messenger of the gods and the source of all speech. Jupiter did not refuse her, and so she gave Mercury these instructions: "Brother Mercury, I never achieved anything without your help, and surely you know I have been looking for this wretched mortal girl. Put out a description and announce a reward for anyone who captures her. I don't want anyone who hides her to be able to say they were ignorant."

And Mercury was quick to do as she asked, stirring up even more interest by adding that anyone giving information leading to Psyche's arrest would receive seven kisses from Venus herself and an eighth kiss sweetened by her tongue. This announcement sent almost the entire male population out looking for Psyche, but it was too late, she was already at Venus' door.

She was met there by Habit, one of the servants, who immediately began screaming abuse at her, grabbed her by the hair, and dragged her to Venus. The goddess broke into near-hysterical laughter, as people sometimes do when they can't control their anger. "So, you've decided to pay a call on your mother-in-law have you? Or is it your wounded husband you came to see? Anyway, I have a reception planned for you." She called for two more of her servants, Care and Misery, and these tortured Psyche while Venus looked on. "Look at that swollen belly," Venus jeered. "Perhaps she hopes we shall feel sorry for her. How happy I am that at my tender age I shall be a grandmother, and that the brat of a slave-girl will be known as my grandson. Fortunately though, the law will not recognize this marriage because it did not take place between equals and it was held in private without witnesses. So the child, if we allow it to be born at all, will be illegitimate."

And Venus flew at her, tore her dress, tugged her hair, and beat her about the head, hurting Psyche quite badly. Then she thought of another humiliation. Gathering every kind of grain and dried vegetable in her house—lentils, limas, millet, black-eyed peas, chick peas, green peas, barley, wheat, and rye—she mixed them all together and dumped them in a great pile on the floor. "You are so hideous," she said, "that the only way you will get a husband is by being a good housekeeper. Sort out this mess, put each grain and bean into its proper pile, and finish the job by this evening." Having given Psyche this impossible task, she went out to a wedding dinner.

Psyche sat motionless staring at the pile, but just then an ant—a regular little black country ant—happened to be passing. He felt sorry for Psyche and hated Venus for her cruelty. Running as fast as he could around the house, he soon gathered an entire army of ants. "Hurry, quick-footed earth-children! Help me save Cupid's wife, a pretty girl in trouble." With incredible speed thousands of ants descended on the pile, sorted it into separate heaps in no time at all, and then vanished.

At dusk Venus returned from her banquet garlanded with roses, soaked in wine, and reeking of perfume. "This is not your work," she said when she saw the neat piles. "Obviously Cupid had a hand in this—so much the worse for you, and for him too." With that she tossed Psyche a piece of bread and went off to bed.

At dawn Venus set the poor girl another impossible task. "See those wild sheep with golden fleeces that graze in the woods by the stream? Bring me a handful of their precious wool at once." Psyche set out rapidly for the stream, not to do what Venus wanted, but to drown herself and put an end to these torments. But for a second time she was prevented. A reed in the stream—the kind that country children use to make whistles—piped up just in time. He advised Psyche to hide under a tree until late afternoon when the sheep generally napped and then gather wool from hedges and branches where it was clinging. She did exactly as he said and returned to Venus with a pile of golden wool gathered in her skirt. But once again the goddess realized that Psyche had been helped, and this time she set an even more difficult test. "Climb that mountain peak and gather for me a flask of water from the black spring that rises there."

Determined that this time no one would stop her killing herself, Psyche set out for the peak, but soon found her way blocked by a massive jagged rock. Rushing torrents burst from dark crevices, and Psyche thought she saw the shapes of snakes darting and writhing in the gloom. In the thunder of the waters she thought she heard voices shouting at her to flee, but her fear petrified her. She stood as still as the stone itself. Yet even in this terrible place Psyche was not without friends. A great eagle who lived in this wild place had once, at Cupid's command, carried the boy Ganymede up from earth to serve as Jupiter's cupbearer. Now he remembered Cupid's power and flew to aid of the girl that the god loved. The eagle knew that this water was sacred, for it was the spring that flowed into the river Styx, the barrier between earth and the underworld of ghosts. Not even Jupiter himself would dare to drink here. But the eagle, pretending he was on a mission from Venus, flew into the chasm and filled the flask.

For the third time Psyche had done what Venus asked, and the goddess had begun to suspect that Psyche was a witch. She was surprised to see her return from the last two tests, but she was sure that Psyche would not come back from what she now asked her to do. "Go down to the underworld. Hand this jar to Proserpina and ask if I can have a little of her beauty—just enough to last for a day — because I am exhausted with caring for my sick son. But don't linger there. I need this before I go to the meeting of the gods tomorrow."

In this way Venus granted Psyche's death wish. She was to cross the river Styx, from whose farthest bank no one had yet returned alive. Eager now to end her misery, she climbed a tower, meaning to throw herself from the top to the rocks below. But the tower itself, like the ant, the eagle, and the reed in the stream, seemed unable to bear the thought that Psyche would die. The stones themselves cried out just in time to stop her. "Don't jump! This is the last of the tests. If you die now you will go to Hades all right, but how will you ever return? Go to the city of Sparta. Near there you will find, in the side of a mountain, a passageway to the underworld. Once you take that route there is no turning back, and don't go empty-handed. Hold in each hand a piece of barley cake soaked in wine, and put two coins in your mouth. When you have almost finished the journey to death, you will meet on the road a lame donkey carrying wood, driven by a lame man. He will ask you to pick up some sticks from the road, but there is no help or pity in the kingdom of death. Pass by without a word.

"Soon after, you will reach the river Styx, where Charon the ferry keeper collects the toll and carries the dead across the water. You will see that even the dead are greedy, and Charon, powerful god though he is, will do nothing without pay. The poorest people have to find their fare. If they don't, they are left waiting at the bank forever. So give the old goat one of your coins, but make him take it from your mouth himself. Remember, give no help to anyone, not even the corpse of an old man that will suddenly float to the surface as you cross the river. He will raise a rotting arm and ask you to pull him in, but ignore him too. Look at death with a cold eye. There is no pity in Hades.

"Then an old woman weaving at a loom will ask for help. Ignore her, too, and keep tight hold on those two cakes. Lose either of them and you will never see daylight again. Finally you will see an enormous three-headed dog who guards the gates of Proserpina's palace. He does not scare the dead—they are beyond fear—but you will be terrified. Throw him a cake, and go quickly in to Proserpina. She will greet you politely and ask you to dinner. Refuse her dinner, sit on the bare floor, and ask for a piece of bread. Then ask her for the jar of beauty, take it, and leave. Use your last barley cake on the dog; your coin will pay Charon's toll for the return crossing, and then at last you will glimpse the stars at the end of the way. One thing more I will tell you—the most important of all—do not look in that jar, and don't be curious about divine beauty."

So it all happened just as the stones said it would. Proserpina turned her back and filled the jar, and Psyche hurried back to the daylight. But as she emerged from the darkness her curiosity got the better of her. "It would be foolish not to take some of this beauty while I have the chance," she thought. "Maybe it will help me to please Cupid." In an instant she removed the lid, but it was empty. Immediately Psyche was overcome by a deep sleep. She simply collapsed where she stood and lay on the path as if she were dead.

Cupid had done little all this time but lie recovering from his wound, but now he could bear his captivity no longer. He slipped out of the window of the bedroom where Venus had locked him up and flew quickly on his rested wings to Psyche. He wiped the sleep from her eyes, returned it to the jar, and woke her with a harmless prick from one of his arrows. "See how near you came to disaster because of that curiosity of yours," he said. "Now go quickly and bring the jar to Venus. I will take care of the rest."

The god still feared his mother, but he was sick with love for Psyche and desperation made him bold and sly. He flew to heaven, knelt before Jupiter's throne, and begged for his help. The great god smiled and kissed him. "It shames me to admit that I, who rule the stars and the planets, have never been able to control you. You have treated me rudely and disrespectfully, wounding me with your arrows, infecting me with human failings, and spreading rumors that I took advantage of various earthwomen while disguised as a bull, a bird, and god knows what other animals. But because I have a kind heart and bounced you on my knee when you were a boy, I will do what you ask—as long as you do me a favor in return. If you happen to know of any woman of outstanding beauty on earth you must introduce me to her."

Having sealed this bargain he put on his godly manner once again, summoned Mercury, and called an immediate council of the gods, threatening that any absentee would be fined. From his throne he made this solemn pronouncement: "Oh Gods, you who the Muses praise! You know I raised this boy, and you know of the scandals caused by his constant immorality. It is time to end his adventures. He chose a girl and made her pregnant. Let his fate be to stay with her forever!"

And then he turned to Venus and said, "Cheer up, my dear. Don't be afraid that your distinguished family will be humbled by association with the girl. I will make her immortal and legalize the marriage."

And so he asked Mercury to bring Psyche immediately to heaven, handed her a cup of ambrosia, the divine drink of the gods, and said, "Drink this, Psyche. It will make you immortal. Cupid will never leave your arms. Your marriage will last to eternity."

And instantly a wedding feast appeared. Cupid reclined with Psyche in his arms, Jupiter and Juno sat together, and all the other gods took their places according to rank and seniority. Much nectar was drunk, the Graces sprinkled sweet-smelling flowers, Apollo played his lyre, and the Muses sang while Venus danced. Even Pan was there, playing his pipes.

So it was that Cupid and Psyche were properly married, and when her time was come a child was born to them. It was not a boy as everyone had expected, but a girl, and they called her Pleasure.

COMMENT: This tale of Cupid and Psyche is translated from the Latin of Apuleius' rambling, picaresque work, *Metamorphoses*, often called *The Golden Ass*. The Roman writer, lecturer, philosopher, and lawyer Lucius Apuleius was born about 123 A.D. at Madaurus in present-day Algeria. We do not know to what degree the tale was invented by Apuleius, but certainly he brought a literary form to an existing body of folklore. His mythical figures, often in new costumes, were borrowed from the Greeks, but the idea of a mysterious husband who comes only in darkness is older still, as is the story of a woman who undergoes terrible ordeals to win her beloved. The motifs that Apuleius uses are both ancient and familiar. It is no surprise to encounter in the first lines the king and queen who had three beautiful daughters, and then to find that two of them turn out to be jealous and spiteful. These elements, like the general confidence that Psyche will somehow win through, tell us that we are reading a fairy tale in the guise of a myth.

The Serpent and the Grape-Grower's Daughter

French

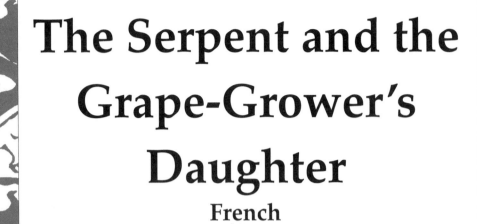

A man was cultivating his vineyard. As he was picking up stones he saw a large one and began to pick it up also. What was his surprise to discover a hole out of which a big serpent came! He was greatly afraid.

The serpent spoke to him. "Who gave you permission to remove the door to my house?"

The man excused himself by saying that he would never have taken that stone to be the door of a house.

Then the serpent answered him. "I know that you have three marriageable daughters. If you don't give me one of the three I'll come at night to crush you. Begone, and give me your reply shortly."

As he went home the man was sad, so very sad that his daughters asked him what the cause of his sorrow was, and he explained to them that, while he was working in the vineyard, moving a big stone, a serpent came out of a hole that it covered and said to him, "Who gave you permission to remove the door to my house?" And he had excused himself by saying that he would never have taken that stone to be the door to a house and that the serpent had answered, "I know that you have three marriageable daughters, and if you don't give me one of the three I'll come at night to crush you. Begone, and give me your reply shortly."

Then the eldest of his daughters cried that she would never be the wife of a serpent, and the next one made the same answer. The youngest alone consoled her father by telling him not to worry, and she assured him that she would make this sacrifice. So the father took the youngest of his daughters by the hand and went with her into the vineyard.

The serpent was waiting for them there at the entrance to his hole. From the threshold he invited them to come down underground, and he led them, crawling on his stomach, and the father and daughter followed him. Soon they arrived in a marvelous castle whose doors opened on magnificent apartments with walls that were upholstered in diamonds, furnished with beautiful furniture, and lighted by resplendent chandeliers. The father and the daughter were surprised to see such beautiful things and the girl was so astounded that she turned toward her father to tell him that she would be happy to become the serpent's wife.

At once they came to an understanding concerning the marriage. The serpent offered to his fiancée a white wedding dress and a dress to wear thereafter. The marriage took place. People of the highest society attended. They went to the church ceremony, and the bride was dressed in her white dress, which had a long train, and the serpent crawled beside her. After the marriage the guests went to the castle where there was a great banquet at which delicious and rare morsels were served, such as pheasants cooked on the skewer over a wood fire. Footmen in livery served.

That evening when all of the guests had withdrawn, the girl followed her husband into her bedroom, but she was horrified to find herself without relatives, without friends, and a serpent beside her. He, seeing her fright, reassured her by explaining to her that he could become a man when he chose, either day or night. Immediately he asked her to say when she desired that he become a man. His wife replied that she preferred him to be a man at night, for thus she would be less terrified; by day she would have less fear than by night to have a beast near her. So the serpent took off his skin immediately, hung it on a nail near his bed, and appeared to her as a beautiful prince who had been bewitched by an evil fairy. The fairy had cast this fate upon him, hoping that he would never succeed in getting married. The next morning he put his snakeskin back on, and so every night he was a prince and every morning a serpent.

A few days later the bride went to visit her parents. Her sisters were jealous of her, seeing her clothed so sumptuously with lovely dresses covered with diamonds. And they suggested that they come to visit her in her castle. And they went and spent a few days with her. She showed them all her beautiful wardrobe and her fine diamonds. They asked her if she wasn't afraid at having a big serpent beside her. Her husband had told her that if one day she invited her sisters, she should be careful not to touch the skin while he was sleeping, that otherwise a great misfortune would befall the two of them. When the young married woman brought her sisters into their bedroom to answer their worried curiosity and to show them that her husband was a handsome prince, she warned them about what her husband had told her. If she invited them one day, they should at least be careful not to touch his skin while he was sleeping. Otherwise a great misfortune would befall the two of them.

Nevertheless the eldest sister, seeing such a handsome prince, was filled with jealousy. To see him closer she had taken a torch in her hand and she approached the serpent's skin out of sheer spite. It was consumed in flames. The prince woke up with a start and said quickly to his wife that she should have remembered the advice he had given her. Immediately to punish her sisters he touched both of them with a magic wand. The two sisters then found themselves outside the castle in the countryside, from which they returned to their home.

The prince said to his wife, "You did not heed my advice, I must punish you, too. Take seven empty bottles and seven pairs of iron shoes. When you have filled these seven bottles with your tears and when you have worn out the seven pairs of shoes, you may come back to me."

Then he touched her with his magic wand and she was in the open countryside alone and lost. She cried night and day and walked unceasingly. She was all the more afflicted and her wandering was all the more painful in that she was with child.

At the end of several months she gave birth to a beautiful son. She fed herself on what she encountered on her way; she ate grass and fruit, and she succeeded thus in staying alive and in feeding her baby. She walked unceasingly for seven years and filled one bottle with her tears each year and used up in the same amount of time one of the pairs of iron shoes. She was all in rags.

At the end of seven years of wandering she saw a village and heard the bells that were ringing as loud as they could. She asked the first person that she met what the big festival was and the reply came, "It's a prince who's getting married. He lost his wife seven years ago. He is remarrying today."

Then the serpent's wife took her baby by the hand and went and stood at the door of the church. Her husband, who recognized her, was overjoyed, stopped on the threshold, and said to all of those in attendance, "I had a pretty key that I lost seven years ago. Today I have recovered it. What must I do? Keep the old one or have a new one made?"

And all of them replied, "If you were satisfied with the old one, why should you have a new one made?"

And they shouted, "Keep the old one!"

Then the prince said, "Here is my wife, whom I have found after seven years. I am taking her back."

And he took her into his beautiful castle, where they lived happily.

COMMENT: "The Serpent and the Grape-Grower's Daughter" is an example of the interchange between—and coexistence of—oral and literary traditions. Collected in 1893 from Madame Ferrié, a sixty-year-old illiterate woman from La Nouvelle, Aude, this French folktale is much simpler and less formal than either Beaumont's "Beauty and the Beast "or Apuleius' "Cupid and Psyche," but it incorporates elements of both. The mysterious Beast/God of the literary tales is replaced by a down-to-earth snake, which has always inspired fear and symbolized sexuality. The concluding key-and-lock motif often appears as a resolution to Cupid and Psyche tales.

The Singing, Soaring Lark

German

*T*here was once upon a time a man who was about to set out on a long journey, and on parting he asked his three daughters what he should bring back with him for them. The eldest wished for pearls, the second wished for diamonds, but the third said, "Dear father, I should like a singing, soaring lark." The father said, "Yes, if I can get it, you shall have it," kissed all three, and set out. Now when the time had come for him to be on his way home again, he had bought pearls and diamonds for the two eldest, but he had sought everywhere in vain for a singing, soaring lark for the youngest, and he was very unhappy about it, for she was his favorite child.

His road lay through a forest, and in the midst of it was a splendid castle, and near the castle stood a tree, but quite on the top of the tree he saw a singing, soaring lark. "Aha, you come just at the right moment!" he said, quite delighted, and called to his servant to climb up and catch the little creature. But as he approached the tree a lion leapt from beneath it, shook himself, and roared till the leaves on the tree trembled. "He who tries to steal my singing, soaring lark," he cried, "will I devour." Then the man said, "I did not know that the bird belonged to you. I will make amends for the wrong I have done and ransom myself with a large sum of money, only spare my life."

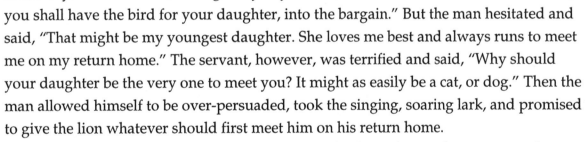

The lion said, "Nothing can save you, unless you will promise to give me what first meets you on your return home. If you will do that, I will grant you your life, and you shall have the bird for your daughter, into the bargain." But the man hesitated and said, "That might be my youngest daughter. She loves me best and always runs to meet me on my return home." The servant, however, was terrified and said, "Why should your daughter be the very one to meet you? It might as easily be a cat, or dog." Then the man allowed himself to be over-persuaded, took the singing, soaring lark, and promised to give the lion whatever should first meet him on his return home.

When he reached home and entered his house, the first who met him was no other than his youngest and dearest daughter, who ran up and kissed and embraced him, and when she saw that he had brought with him a singing, soaring lark, she was beside herself with joy. The father, however, could not rejoice, but began to weep and said, "My dearest child, I have bought the little bird dear. In return for it, I have been obliged to promise you to a savage lion, and when he has you he will tear you in pieces and devour you." And he told her all, just as it had happened, and begged her not to go there, come what might. But she consoled him and said, "Dearest father, indeed your promise must be fulfilled. I will go thither and soften the lion, so that I may return to you safely."

Next morning she had the road pointed out to her, took leave, and went fearlessly out into the forest. The lion, however, was an enchanted prince and was by day a lion, and all his people were lions with him, but in the night they resumed their natural human shapes. On her arrival she was kindly received and led into the castle. When night came, the lion turned into a handsome man, and their wedding was celebrated with great magnificence. They lived happily together, remained awake at night, and slept in the daytime.

One day he came and said, "Tomorrow there is a feast in your father's house, because the eldest sister is to be married, and if you are inclined to go there, my lions shall conduct you." She said, "Yes, I should very much like to see my father again," and went thither, accompanied by the lions. There was great joy when she arrived, for they had all believed that she had been torn in pieces by the lion and long ceased to live. But she told them what a handsome husband she had and how well-off she was. She remained with them while the wedding feast lasted and then went back to the forest.

When the second daughter was about to be married and the youngest daughter was again invited to the wedding, she said to the lion, "This time I will not be alone, you must come with me." The lion, however, said that it was too dangerous for him, for if, when he was there, a ray from a burning candle fell on him, he would be changed into a dove, and for seven years long would have to fly about with the doves. She said, "Ah, but do come with me. I will take great care of you and guard you from all light." So they went away together and took with them their small child as well. The prince's wife had a chamber built there, so strong and thick that no ray could pierce through it; in this he was to shut himself up when the candles were lit for the wedding feast. But the door was made of green wood, which warped and left a little crack that no one noticed. The wedding was celebrated with magnificence, but when the procession with all its candles and torches came back from the church and passed by this apartment, a ray about the breadth of a hair fell on the prince, and when this ray touched him, he was transformed in an instant. When the prince's wife came in and looked for him, she did not see him, but a white dove was sitting there. The dove said to her, "For seven years must I fly about the world, but at every seventh step that you take, I will let fall a drop of red. blood and a white feather, and I will show you the way. If you follow the trail you can release me." Thereupon the dove flew out the door and she followed him. At every seventh step a red drop of blood and a little white feather fell down and showed her the way.

So she went continually further and further in the wide world, never looking about her or resting, and the seven years were almost past. Then she rejoiced and thought that they would soon be delivered, and yet they were far from it! Once when they were moving onward, no little feather and no drop of red blood fell, and when she raised her eyes the dove had disappeared. And as she thought to herself, "In this no man can help me," she climbed up to the sun and said to him, "You shine into every crevice, and over every peak; haven't you seen a white dove flying?"

"No," said the sun, "I have seen none, but I present you with a casket. Open it when you are in sorest need." She thanked the sun and went on until evening came and the moon appeared, whereupon she asked her, "You shine the whole night through and on every field and forest. Haven't you seen a white dove flying?" "No," said the moon, "I have seen no dove, but here I give you an egg. Break it when you are in great need." She thanked the moon and went on until the night wind came up and blew on her. Then she said to it, "You blow over every tree and under every leaf, haven't you seen a white dove flying?" "No," said the night wind, "I have seen none, but I will ask the three other winds. Perhaps they have seen it." The east wind and the west wind came and had seen nothing, but the south wind said, "I have seen the white dove. It has flown to the Red Sea, and there it has become a lion again, for the seven years are over, and the lion is there fighting with a dragon. The dragon, however, is an enchanted princess."

The night wind then said to her, "I will advise you. Go to the Red Sea. On the right bank are some tall reeds. Count them, break off the eleventh, and strike the dragon with it, then the lion will be able to subdue it, and both then will regain their human form. After that, look round and you will see a griffin by the Red Sea. Swing yourself, with your beloved, on his back, and the bird will carry you over the sea to your own home. Here is a nut for you. When you are above the center of the sea, let the nut fall. It will immediately shoot up, and out of the water a tall nut tree will grow on which the griffin may rest; for if he cannot rest, he will not be strong enough to carry you across, and if you forget to throw down the nut, he will let you fall into the sea."

Then she went thither and found everything as the night wind had said. She counted the reeds by the sea, cut off the eleventh, and struck the dragon, whereupon the lion overcame it, and immediately both of them regained their human shapes. But when the princess, who had before been the dragon, was delivered from enchantment, she took the youth by the arm, seated herself on the griffin, and carried him off with her. There stood the poor maiden who had wandered so far and was again forsaken. She sat down and cried, but at last she took courage and said, "Still I will go as far as the wind blows and as long as the cock crows, until I find him." And she went forth by long, long roads, until at last she came to the castle where both of them were living together.

There she heard that soon a feast was to be held in which they would celebrate their wedding, but she said, "God still helps me," and opened the casket that the sun had given her. A dress lay therein as brilliant as the sun itself. So she took it out and put it on and went up into the castle, and everyone, even the bride herself, looked at her with astonishment. The dress pleased the bride so well that she thought it might do for her wedding dress, and asked if it was for sale. "Not for money or land," answered she, "but for flesh and blood." The bride asked her what she meant by that, and she said, "Let me sleep a night in the chamber where the bridegroom sleeps."

The bride would not, yet wanted very much to have the dress. At last she consented, but the page was to give the prince a sleeping potion. When it was night, therefore, and the youth was already asleep, she was led into the chamber. She seated herself on the bed and said, "I have followed after you for seven years. I have been to the sun and the moon and the four winds and have inquired for you and have helped you against the dragon. Will you, then, quite forget me?" But the prince slept so soundly that it only seemed to him as if the wind were whistling outside in the fir trees. When day broke, she was led out again and had to give up the golden dress. And as even that had been of no avail, she was sad, went out into a meadow, sat down there, and wept.

While she was sitting there, she thought of the egg that the moon had given her. She opened it, and out came a clucking hen with twelve chickens all of gold, and they ran about chirping and crept again under the old hen's wings. Nothing more beautiful was ever seen in the world! Then she arose and drove them through the meadow before her until the bride looked out of the window. The little chickens pleased her so much that she immediately came down and asked if they were for sale. "Not for money or land, but for flesh and blood. Let me sleep another night in the chamber where the bride-groom sleeps." The bride said, "Yes," intending to cheat her as on the former evening. But when the prince went to bed, he asked the page what the murmuring and rustling in the night had been. On this, the page told all; that he had been forced to give him a sleeping potion because a poor girl had slept secretly in the chamber and that he was to give him another that night. The prince said, "Pour out the potion by the bedside."

At night, she was again led in, and when she began to relate how badly she had fared, he immediately recognized his beloved wife by her voice, sprang up, and cried, "Now I truly am released! I have been as if in a dream, for the strange princess has bewitched me so that I have been compelled to forget you, but God has delivered me from the spell at the right time." Then they both left the castle secretly in the night, for they feared the father of the princess, who was a sorcerer, and they seated themselves on the griffin, which bore them across the Red Sea, and when they were in the midst of it, she let fall the nut. Immediately a tall nut tree grew up. The bird rested and then carried them home, where they found their child, who had grown tall and beautiful, and they lived thenceforth happily until their death.

COMMENT: Like the lamp that burns Cupid's shoulder and sends him flying away from Psyche, a candle ray turns the lion prince of this German variant into a dove, forcing the heroine to go on a quest for her husband and win him away from a dragon princess as powerful as Venus. Since the heroine must undergo physical tests to save her lover, the tale is clearly closer to the "Cupid and Psyche" tale type than to "Beauty and the Beast." "The Singing, Soaring Lark" or "The Lilting, Leaping Lark," as it is sometimes translated, was first published in 1812 by the Grimm brothers, Jakob and Wilhelm, in their famous collection *Kinder- und Hausmärchen*. Like the storytellers who told them the tales, the Grimms adapted and changed what they passed on. Their interest in nationalizing a language and folk heritage led them to impose their own story patterns on what they heard and wrote down.

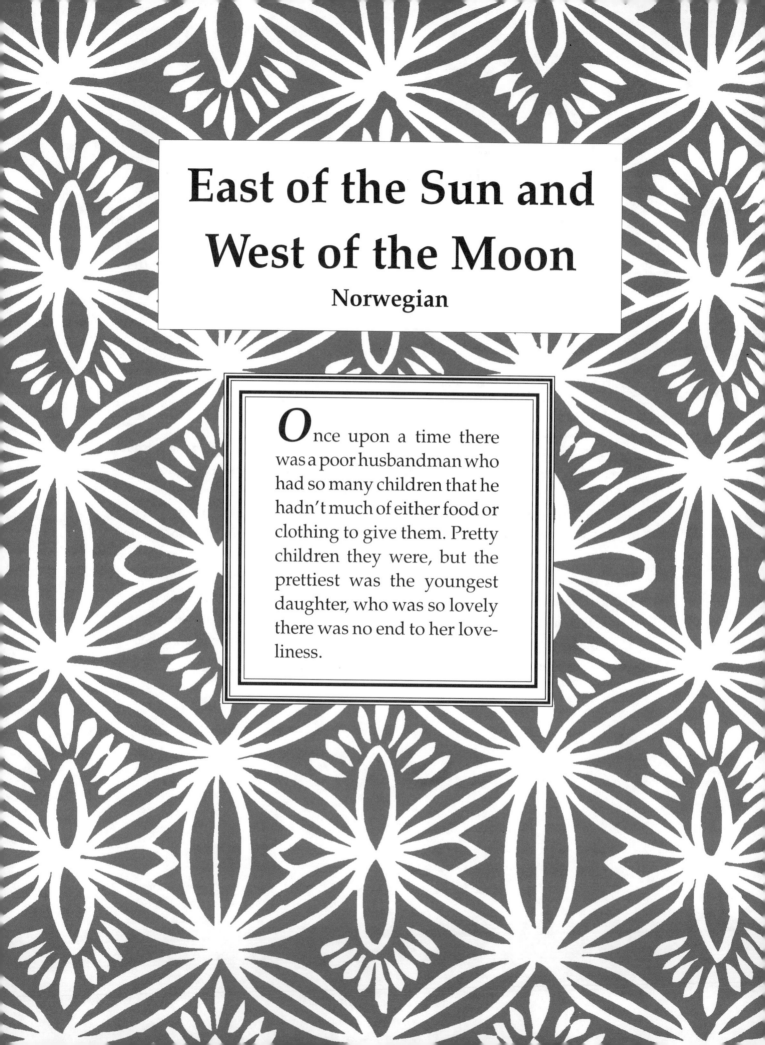

East of the Sun and West of the Moon

Norwegian

*O*nce upon a time there was a poor husbandman who had so many children that he hadn't much of either food or clothing to give them. Pretty children they were, but the prettiest was the youngest daughter, who was so lovely there was no end to her loveliness.

So one day, 'twas on a Thursday evening late at the fall of the year, the weather was so wild and rough outside, and it was so cruelly dark and rain fell and wind blew till the walls of the cottage shook again. There they all sat round the fire busy with this thing and that. But just then, all at once something gave three taps on the windowpane. Then the father went out to see what was the matter and when he got out of doors, what should he see but a great big White Bear.

"Good evening to you," said the White Bear.

"The same to you," said the man.

"Will you give me your youngest daughter? If you will, I'll make you as rich as you are now poor," said the Bear.

Well, the man would not be at all sorry to be so rich, but still he thought he must have a bit of a talk with his daughter first. So he went in and told them how there was a great White Bear waiting outside who had given his word to make them so rich if he could only have the youngest daughter.

The lassie said "No!" outright. Nothing could get her to say anything else, so the man went out and settled it with the White Bear that he should come again the next Thursday evening and get an answer. Meantime he talked to his daughter and kept on telling her of all the riches they would get and how well off she would be herself. At last she thought better of it and washed and mended her rags, made herself as smart as she could, and was ready to start. I can't say her packing gave her much trouble.

Next Thursday evening came the White Bear to fetch her, and she got upon his back with her bundle, and off they went. So, when they had gone a bit of the way, the White Bear said, "Are you afraid?"

No, she wasn't.

"Well, mind and hold tight by my shaggy coat, and then there's nothing to fear," said the Bear.

So she rode a long, long way, till they came to a great, steep hill. There, on the face of it, the White Bear gave a knock, a door opened, and they came into a castle, where there were many rooms all lit up, rooms gleaming with silver and gold and there too was a table ready laid, and it was all as grand as grand could be. Then the White Bear gave her a silver bell. When she wanted anything, she was only to ring it and she would get it at once.

Well, after she had eaten and drunk and evening wore on, she got sleepy from her journey and thought she would like to go to bed, so she rang the bell. She had hardly taken hold of it before she came into a chamber where there was a bed made, as fair and white as anyone would wish to sleep in, with silken pillows, curtains, and gold fringe. All that was in the room was gold or silver. When she had gone to bed and put out the light, a man came and laid himself alongside her. That was the White Bear, who threw off his beast shape at night. But she never saw him, for he always came after she had put out the light, and before the day dawned he was up and off again. So things went on happily for a while, but at last she began to get silent and sorrowful. For there she went about all day alone, and she longed to go home to see her father and mother and brothers and sisters. So one day, when the White Bear asked what it was that she lacked, she said it was so dull and lonely there, and she longed to go home to see her father and mother and brothers and sisters, and that was why she was so sad and sorrowful, because she couldn't get to them.

"Well, well!" said the Bear. "Perhaps there's a cure for all this. You must promise me one thing. Do not talk alone with your mother, but only when the rest are by to hear. For she'll take you by the hand and try to lead you into a room alone to talk. But you must mind and not do that, else you'll bring bad luck on both of us."

So one Sunday the White Bear came and said now they could set off to see her father and mother. Well, off they started, she sitting on his back; and they went far and long. At last they came to a grand house, and there her brothers and sisters were running about out of doors at play, and everything was so pretty 'twas a joy to see.

"This is where your father and mother live now," said the White Bear, "but don't forget what I told you, else you'll make us both unlucky."

No, bless her, she'd not forget, and when she had reached the house, the White Bear turned right about and left her.

Then when she went in to see her father and mother there was such joy, there was no end to it. None of them thought they could thank her enough for all she had done for them. Now they had everything they wished, as good as good could be, and they all wanted to know how she got on where she lived.

Well, she said, it was very good to live where she did; she had all she wished. What she said beside I don't know. But I don't think any of them had the right end of the stick, or that they got much out of her. So in the afternoon, after they had done dinner, all happened as the White Bear had said. Her mother wanted to talk with her alone in her bedroom, but she minded what the White Bear had said and wouldn't go upstairs.

"Oh, what we have to talk about will keep," she said, and put her mother off. But somehow or other, her mother got round her at last, and she had to tell her the whole story. So she said how every night when she had gone to bed, a man came and lay down beside her as soon as she had put out the light; how she never saw him, because he was always up and away before the morning dawned; how she went about woeful and sorrowing, for she thought she should so like to see him; how all day long she walked about there alone; and how dull, dreary, and lonesome it was.

"My!" said her mother. "It may well be a Troll you slept with! But now I'll teach you a lesson on how to set eyes on him. I'll give you a bit of candle, which you can carry home in your bosom. Just light that while he is asleep, but take care not to drop the tallow on him."

Yes! She took the candle and hid it in her bosom, and as night drew on, the White Bear came and fetched her away.

But when they had gone a bit of the way, the White Bear asked if all hadn't happened as he had said.

Well, she couldn't say it hadn't.

"Now, mind," said he, "if you have listened to your mother's advice, you have brought bad luck on us both and then all that has passed between us will be as nothing."

"No," she said, she hadn't listened to her mother's advice.

So when she reached home and had gone to bed, it was the same old story over again. There came a man who lay down beside her, but at dead of night, when she heard he slept, she got up and struck a light, lit the candle, and let the light shine on him, and so she saw that he was the loveliest Prince one ever set eyes on. She fell so deep in love with him on the spot that she thought she couldn't live if she didn't give him a kiss there and then. And so she did, but as she kissed him, she dropped three hot drops of tallow on his shirt, and he woke up.

"What have you done?" he cried. "Now you have made us both unlucky, for had you held out only this one year, I would have been freed. For I have a stepmother who has bewitched me so that I am a White Bear by day and a Man by night. But now all ties are snapped between us; now I must set off from you to her. She lives in a castle which stands east o' the sun and west o' the moon, and there, too, is a Princess, with a nose three ells long, and she's the wife I must have now."

She wept and took it ill, but there was no help for it; go he must.

Then she asked if she mightn't go with him.

No, she mightn't.

"Tell me the way, then," she said, "and I'll search you out. *That* surely I may get leave to do."

"Yes, you might do that," he said. But there was no way to that place. It lay east o' the sun and west o' the moon, and thither she'd never find her way.

So next morning, when she woke up, both Prince and castle were gone, and she lay on a little green patch in the midst of the gloomy thick wood, and by her side lay the same bundle of rags she had brought with her from her old home.

So when she had rubbed the sleep out of her eyes and wept till she was tired, she set out on her way and walked many, many days, till she came to a lofty crag. Under it sat an old hag who played with a gold apple. Her the lassie asked if she knew the way to the Prince, who lived with his stepmother in the castle that lay east o' the sun and west o' the moon, and who was to marry the Princess with a nose three ells long.

"How did you come to know about him?" asked the old hag. "But maybe you are the lassie who ought to have had him?"

Yes, she was.

"So, so. It's you, is it?" said the old hag. "Well, all I know about him is that he lives in the castle that lies east o' the sun and west o' the moon, and thither you'll come, later or never. But still you may have the loan of my horse, and on him you can ride to my next neighbor. Maybe she'll be able to tell you. And when you get there, just give the horse a switch under the left ear and beg him to be off home. Wait, this gold apple you may take with you."

So she got up on the horse and rode a long, long time, till she came to another crag, under which sat another old hag with a gold carding-comb. Her the lassie asked if she knew the way to the castle that lay east o' the sun and west o' the moon, and she answered, like the first old hag, that she knew nothing about it, except it was east o' the sun and west o' the moon.

"And thither you'll come, late or never, but you shall have the loan of my horse to my next neighbor. Maybe she'll tell you all about it. And when you get there, just switch the horse under the left ear and beg him to be off home."

East of the Sun and West of the Moon

And this old hag gave her the golden carding-comb. It might be she'd find some use for it, she said. So the lassie got up on the horse and rode a far far way, a weary time. At last she came to another great crag, under which sat another old hag, spinning with a golden spinning-wheel. Her, too, she asked if she knew the way to the Prince and where the castle was that lay east o' the sun and west o' the moon. So it was the same thing over again.

"Maybe it's you who ought to have had the Prince?" said the old hag.

Yes, it was.

But she, too, didn't know the way a bit better than the other two. "East o' the sun and west o' the moon it was," she knew—that was all.

"And thither you'll come, later or never, but I'll lend you my horse, and then I think you'd best ride to the East Wind and ask him. Maybe he knows those parts and can blow you thither. But when you get to him, you need only give the horse a switch under the left ear, and he'll trot home of himself."

And so, too, she gave her the gold spinning-wheel. "Maybe you'll find a use for it," said the old hag.

Then she rode many many days, a weary time, before she got to the East Wind's house. But at last she did reach it, and then she asked the East Wind if he could tell her the way to the Prince who dwelt east o' the sun and west o' the moon. Yes, the East Wind had often heard tell of it, the Prince and the castle, but he couldn't tell the way, for he had never blown so far.

"But, if you will, I'll go with you to my brother the West Wind. Maybe he knows, for he's much stronger. So, if you will just get on my back, I'll carry you thither."

Yes, she got on his back, and I should just think they went briskly along.

So when they got there, they went into the West Wind's house, and the East Wind said the lassie he had brought was the one who ought to have had the Prince who lived in the castle east o' the sun and west o' the moon, and so she had set out to seek him. He had come with her and would be glad to know if the West Wind knew how to get to the castle.

"Nay," said the West Wind, "so far I've never blown. But if you will, I'll go with you to our brother the South Wind, for he's much stronger than either of us, and he has flapped his wings far and wide. Maybe he'll tell you. You can get on my back, and I'll carry you to him."

Yes! She got on his back, and so they traveled to the South Wind and weren't so very long on the way, I should think.

When they got there, the West Wind asked him if he could tell her the way to the castle that lay east o' the sun and west o' the moon, for it was she who ought to have had the Prince who lived there.

"You don't say so! That's she, is it?" said the South Wind.

"Well, I have blustered about in most places in my time, but so far have I never blown. But if you will, I'll take you to my brother the North Wind. He is the oldest and strongest of the whole lot of us, and if he doesn't know where it is, you'll never find anyone in the world to tell you. You can get on my back, and I'll carry you thither."

Yes! She got on his back, and away he went from his house at a fine rate. And this time, too, she wasn't long on her way.

So when they got to the North Wind's house, he was so wild and cross, cold puffs came from him a long way off.

"BLAST YOU BOTH, WHAT DO YOU WANT?" he roared out to them ever so far off, so that it struck them with an icy shiver.

"Well," said the South Wind, "you needn't be so foul-mouthed, for here I am, your brother, the South Wind, and here is the lassie who ought to have had the Prince who dwells in the castle that lies east o' the sun and west o' the moon. She wants to ask you if you ever were there and can tell her the way, for she would be so glad to find him again."

"YES, I KNOW WELL ENOUGH WHERE IT IS," said the North Wind. "Once in my life I blew an aspen-leaf thither, but I was so tired I couldn't blow a puff for ever so many days after. But if you really wish to go thither, and aren't afraid to come along with me, I'll take you on my back and see if I can blow you thither."

Yes! With all her heart; she must and would get thither if it were possible in any way; and as for fear, however madly he went, she wouldn't be at all afraid.

"Very well, then," said the North Wind. "But you must sleep here tonight, for we must have the whole day before us, if we're to get thither at all."

Early next morning the North Wind woke her and puffed himself up, blew himself out, and made himself so stout and big, 'twas gruesome to look at him. And so off they went high up through the air, as if they would never stop till they got to the world's end.

Down here below there was such a storm; it threw down long tracts of wood and many houses, and when it swept over the great sea, ships foundered by hundreds.

So they tore on and on—no one can believe how far they went—and all the while they still went over the sea, and the North Wind got more and more weary and so out of breath he could scarce bring out a puff, and his wings drooped and drooped, till at last he sunk so low that the crests of the waves dashed over his heels.

"Are you afraid?" said the North Wind.

"No!" She wasn't.

But they weren't very far from land, and the North Wind had still so much strength left in him that he managed to throw her up on the shore under the windows of the castle that lay east o' the sun and west o' the moon. He was so weak and worn out, he had to stay there and rest many days before he could get home again.

Next morning the lassie sat down under the castle window and began to play with the gold apple. The first person she saw was the Long-nose who was to have the Prince.

"What do you want for your gold apple, you lassie?" said the Long-nose, and threw up the window.

"It's not for sale, for gold or money," said the lassie.

"If it's not for sale for gold or money, what is it that you will sell it for? You may name your own price," said the Princess.

"Well! If I may get to the Prince, who lives here, and be with him tonight, you shall have it," said the lassie whom the North Wind had brought.

Yes! She might; that could be done. So the Princess got the gold apple. But when the lassie came up to the Prince's bedroom at night he was fast asleep. She called him and shook him and between while she wept sore, but all she could do couldn't wake him up. Next morning as soon as day broke came the Princess with the long nose and drove her out again.

So in the daytime she sat down under the castle windows and began to card with her golden carding-comb, and the same thing happened. The Princess asked what she wanted for it, and she said it wasn't for sale for gold or money, but if she might get leave to go up to the Prince and be with him that night, the Princess should have it. But when she went up she found him fast asleep again, and all she called, and all she shook, and wept, and prayed, she couldn't get life into him. As soon as the first gray peep of day came, then came the Princess with the long nose, and chased her out again.

So in the daytime the lassie sat down outside under the castle window and began to spin with her golden spinning-wheel, and that, too, the Princess with the long nose wanted to have. So she threw up the window and asked what she wanted for it. The lassie said, as she had said twice before, it wasn't for sale for gold or money, but if she might go up to the Prince who was there and be with him alone that night, she might have it.

Yes! She might do that and welcome. But now you must know there were some Christian folk who had been carried off thither, and as they sat in their room, which was next to the Prince, they had heard how a woman had been in there who wept and prayed and called to him two nights running, and they told that to the Prince.

That evening, when the Princess came with her sleepy drink, the Prince made as if he drank, but threw it over his shoulder, for he could guess it was a sleepy drink. So, when the lassie came in, she found the Prince wide awake; and then she told him the whole story of how she had come thither.

"Ah," said the Prince, "you've just come in the very nick of time, for tomorrow is to be our wedding day. But now I won't have the Long-nose, and you are the only woman in the world who can set me free. I'll say I want to see what my wife is fit for, and beg her to wash the shirt which has the three spots of tallow on it. She'll say yes, for she doesn't know 'tis you who put them there. But that's a work only for Christian folk, and not for such a pack of Trolls, and so I'll say that I won't have any other for my bride than the woman who can wash them out, and ask you to do it."

So there was great joy and love between them all that night. But next day, when the wedding was to be, the Prince said, "First of all, I'd like to see what my bride is fit for."

"Yes!" said the stepmother with all her heart.

"Well," said the Prince, "I've got a fine shirt which I'd like for my wedding shirt, but somehow or other it has got three spots of tallow on it, which I must have washed out, and I have sworn never to take any other bride than the woman who's able to do that. If she can't, she's not worth having."

Well, that was no great thing, they said, so they agreed, and she with the long nose began to wash away as hard as she could, but the more she rubbed and scrubbed, the bigger the spots grew.

"Ah!" said the old hag, her mother, "You can't wash. Let me try."

But she hadn't long taken the shirt in hand before it got far worse than ever, and with all her rubbing and wringing and scrubbing, the spots grew bigger and blacker, and the darker and uglier was the shirt.

Then all the other Trolls began to wash, but the longer it lasted, the blacker and uglier the shirt grew, till at last it was as black all over as if it had been up the chimney.

Ah!" said the Prince, "You're none of you worth a straw; you can't wash. Why there, outside, sits a beggar lassie, I'll be bound she knows how to wash better than the whole lot of you. COME IN, LASSIE!" he shouted.

Well, in she came.

"Can you wash this shirt clean, lassie, you?" said he.

"I don't know," she said, "but I think I can."

And almost before she had taken it and dipped it in the water, it was as white as driven snow, and whiter still.

"Yes; you are the lassie for me," said the Prince.

At that the old hag flew into such a rage, she burst on the spot, and the Princess with the long nose after her, and the whole pack of Trolls after her—at least I've never heard a word about them since.

As for the Prince and Princess, they set free all the poor Christian folk who had been carried off and shut up there, and they took with them all the silver and gold and flitted away as far as they could from the castle that lay east o' the sun and west o' the moon.

COMMENT: "East of the Sun and West of the Moon," which first appeared in P.C. Asbjørnsen and J. Moe's collection, *Norske Folke-eventyr* (Christiania, 1843-44 and 1852), was translated from the Norwegian by Sir George Webbe Dasent in *Popular Tales of the Norse* (Edinburgh, 1859). This is perhaps the most famous folk variant of the Cupid and Psyche tale type. Its relationship to Apuleius' Greco-Roman literary tale is clear, but the cast—including a white bear, a powerful north wind, and heathen trolls that imprison good Christian folk—is distinctively Scandanavian. It was this story, which I heard often as a child, that generated my lifelong interest in Beauty and Beast tales. The book from which my mother read to me, and which I later read alone, was this same translation illustrated with the elegant, elongated figures painted by Kay Nielsen.

Whitebear Whittington

Appalachian

*O*ne time there was a man had three daughters. His wife was dead, and the three girls they kept house for him. And one day he was fixin' to go to town, so he called his girls, asked 'em what did they want him to bring 'em. The oldest told him, says, "I want a silk dress the color of every bird in the sky."

The second girl said, "I want you to bring me a silk dress made out of every color in a rainbow."

The youngest 'un she didn't say anything. So directly he went and asked her didn't she want him to bring her something too, and now she studied a minute, says, "All I want is some white roses. If you see a white rosebush anywhere you might break me a basketful."

Well, he took him a basket of eggs and got on his horse and went on to town. Got all his tradin' done and started back. Rode on, rode on, come to where there was a thick wilderness of a palace, saw a big rosebush 'side the road, full of white roses. So he got off his horse and broke off a few. Thought he heard something behind him, says

> *You break them*
> *And I'll break you.*

So he stopped, looked around, waited awhile, and tried to see what it was spoke, didn't see anybody nor hear it again, so he broke off some more. Then he heard it real plain—sounded like it was back in the wilderness—

> *You break them*
> *And I'll break you.*

He started to quit that time, but he still couldn't see anybody or anything and the prettiest roses were still on the bush, so he reached out his hand to break them off—and that thing said:

> *Give me what meets you*
> *first at the gate,*
> *you can break all you want*
> *till your basket is full.*

He thought a minute or two—and he knew that his old dog always came lopin' out in the road whenever he got in home. The old hound wasn't much good anyway—so he answered, says

> *Whatever meets me*
> *first at the gate,*
> *you can come take it*
> *whenever you want.*

Went ahead and broke white rosebuds till his basket was full. Got on his horse and rode on in home.

He kept lookin' for his dog to come out but the old hound was up under the house asleep and before he could whistle for it here came his youngest girl flyin' out the gate to meet him.

He hollered to her and motioned her to go back but she wasn't payin' him any mind, came right on. She took his basket and was a-carryin' on over how pretty the roses were. So she thanked him and went to helpin' him unload his saddlebags, and when they got to the house she saw he was lookin' troubled, says, "What's the matter, Daddy?" But he wouldn't tell her.

And he never came to the table when they called him to supper, just sat there on the porch lookin' back down the holler. So the girls they ate their supper, and it got dark directly and they lit the lamp. Sat there sewin' and talkin', and all at once they heard a voice out in the road—

"Send out my pay!"

Their daddy came in the house then, and told 'em what'n-all he had heard when he broke the roses. The oldest girl she said to him, says, "Aw, just send out the dog. How could it know what met you first?"

So they called the dog and sicced him out toward the gate. He ran out barkin' and then they heard him come back a-howlin', scared to death, and he crawled way back under the floor and stayed there. Then they heard it again—

"Send out my pay!"

So the two oldest girls said they wasn't afraid, said they'd go see what it was. Out they went, and directly there was a commotion at the gate and the two girls came tearin' back to the house so scared they couldn't speak. Then it hollered louder—

"Send out my pay!"

Then the youngest girl said, "I'll have to go, Daddy, but don't you worry; I'll come back some way or other."

So she gathered her up a few things in a budget [small pack] and kissed her father and went on out to the gate. There stood a big white bear.

"Get up on my back," it told her. So she crawled up on its back and it started off.

The girl was cryin' so hard her nose bled and three drops of blood fell on the white bear's back. They went on, went on, and 'way up in the night she made how they went past a big white rosebush out in a thick wilderness. Came to a fine house out there and the white bear stopped, told her, "Get off now."

So she got off and went on in the house. The white bear came in behind her, says, "Light that lamp there on the table." So she lit the lamp, and when she turned back around there stood a good-lookin' young man. The minute she looked at him she thought the world of him. He said to her then says, "This house and everything in it belongs to you now, and there's nothing here to hurt you."

Then he took the lamp and they went through all the rooms lookin' at all the fine things, and directly they came to a pretty bedroom and he told her, says, "Now I got a spell on me and I can't be a man but part of the time. From now on I can be a man of a night and stay with you here and be a bear of a day, or I can be a bear of a night and sleep under your bed and be a man of a day. Which had you rather I'd be?"

So she thought about it and she didn't like the idea of a bear layin' under her bed of a night so she told him she'd rather he'd be a man of a night. So that was the way it was. He was a bear in the daytime and he'd lie around outside while she kept house, and when dark came he'd be a man. He kept plenty of wood and water in the house and they'd talk together and he was good company.

So they kept on. She lived happy even if her husband did have to be a bear half the time. He told her how it was he'd been witched, said he'd get out of it some day but he didn't know just how it would be. And after three or four years she had three little babes, two boys and a girl. Then when her least one was big enough to walk she told her husband she wanted to go back to see her father again. It looked like that troubled him but he told her all right, they would go; but he said she would have to promise him not to tell *any*body anything about him, and *never* to speak his name.

"If you speak my name to any living soul I'll have to go away. And you will see me going off up the mountain and it will be awful hard for us ever to get together again."

So she promised him and early the next mornin' he took her and the three children on his back, and he let them off at her father's gate and she took her babes and went on to the house.

They were all proud to see her again and told her how pretty her children were and commenced askin' her who her husband was and where they lived and all. She told 'em she couldn't tell. Well, they kept on at her and she kept tellin' 'em she couldn't possibly tell, so her sisters they started actin' mad and wouldn't speak to her. Still she wouldn't tell. But the next day her daddy took her aside and spoke to her about it, says, "Just tell me his name."

She thought surely she ought to tell her own father what her man's name was, so she whispered it to him, "Whitebear Whittington."

And she hadn't but spoke it when she looked up and saw her husband and he was in the shape of a man, and he was goin' off up the Piney Mountain, and on the back of his white shirt were three drops of blood.

Well, she loved him, so she left the children there with her father and started out to try and find her man again. She took out the way he went over the Piney Mountain but she never did see him on ahead of her. But she went on and went on. Sometimes she'd think she was lost but a white bird would fly over and drop a white feather with a red speck on it, so she'd go on the way that bird was headed. Then she'd stop at a house to stay the night and they'd tell her about the fine young man had stayed there the night before, had three drops of blood on his shirt.

So she went on, went on, for seven years and that bird would fly over whenever she got downhearted, so she didn't give up. Then late one evening she stopped at a house and called to stay the night and an old, old woman awful stricken in age came to the door, looked like she was over a hundred years old and she was walkin' on two sticks, told her to come on in. The old woman looked at her, says, "Girl, you're in bad trouble, now ain't ye?"

So she told the old lady about what'n-all had happened and how she'd been tryin' to find her man again, and directly the old woman told her, says, "You just stay here with me now, and get rested up a little, and it may be I can help you. I got a lot of wool to work and I need somebody. Will you stay and help me about my wool?"

She said yes, she would. So the next day they got all the fleeces out and she helped pick out the burs and trash and washed the wool in the creek while the old woman carded. Carded so fast the girl had a time keepin' up with her and they got it all done by sundown. And that night the old woman gave her a gold chinquapin [chestnut]. The next day the girl she helped with the spinnin', handed the rolls of carded wool to the old lady, and it was a sight in the world how she could spin. They got it all spun up about dark, and that night the old woman handed her a gold hickory nut. Then the third day the old woman she sat down at her loom and the girl kept fixin' the bobbins and handin' 'em to her and the old loom went *click! wham! click! wham!* all day long, and just 'fore dark the weavin' was all done. So that night the old woman gave her a gold walnut, says, "Now you keep these three gold nuts and don't you crack 'em till you're in the most trouble you could ever be in. And if the first one don't get ye out, crack the next, and if you have to crack the last 'un you surely ought to be out of your trouble by then."

So she thanked the old lady and the next mornin' she left with the three gold nuts in her apron pocket. She went on, went on, and in three days she came to a river and she went along the river till she came to a washin' place where a great crowd of young women were gathered, and there in the middle of all them women she saw her husband. She got through the crowd and went up to him but when he looked at her it was just as if he never had known her before in all his life.

He didn't have any shirt on and she saw the women lined up before the washin' place and one girl was down on her knees washin' his shirt with all her might. She listened and heard 'em talkin' about how that young man had said he'd marry the one could wash the blood out of his shirt. So she got in the line and fin'lly got down to the washin' place. The one ahead of her was a big stout woman and she was down on her knees a-washin' that shirt so hard it looked like she'd tear it apart. Soap it and maul it with the battlin' stick and rinse it and soap it and maul it again, but the blood just got darker and darker. So directly the girl said she'd like to have her turn. That other woman didn't get up off her knees, looked at her, says, "Humph! If I can't get this blood out I know a puny thing like you can't do it."

Well, that girl she just leaned down and took hold on his shirt and gave it one rub and it was white as snow. But before she could turn around the other woman grabbed it and ran with it, says, "Look! Look! I washed it out!"

So the young man he had to go home with her.

His real wife knew now that she was in the most trouble she could ever be in. So she followed 'em and saw what house it was, and about dark she went there, went right in the door and cracked her gold chinquapin. It coiled out the finest gold wool you ever saw—just one long carded roll ready to be spun. So she started pullin' out the gold wool and pretty soon that other woman came and saw it says, "Oh, I must have that! What will you take for it?"

"Why, I couldn't part with my gold nut."

"You name any price you want now, and I'll give it to ye."

"Let me stay this night with your man and you can have it."

"Well! I must have that gold chinquapin. You go on out and wait till I call ye."

So she took the gold chinquapin and put it away. Then she put a sleepy pillow on the young man's bed and just before he went to go to bed she gave him a sleepy dram, and then she called that girl, and when she went in to him he was sound asleep. She sat down beside him and tried to wake him up but he slept right on. So she stayed there by him all night cryin' and singin':

Three drops of blood I've shed for thee!
Three little babes I've born for thee!
Whitebear Whittington! Turn to me!

And when daylight came that other woman made her leave. Well, the girl came back that next evening and broke the gold hickory nut. A fine spinning wheel came out of it, stood right up in the floor and started spinnin'. All you had to do was put the gold chinquapin in a crack in the logs and set the end of the wool on the spindle, and it spun right on—spin and wind, spin and wind all by itself. Hit was the finest gold thread you ever saw. And when that woman came in and saw it, said she just had to have the wheel. So the girl let her have it for another night with her man. But when she went to him he slept right on through the night because that sleepy pillow was still under his head and that woman had gone and given him another sleepy dram. So all night his wife stayed by him tryin' to wake him up.

Three drops of blood I've shed for thee!
Three little babes I've born for thee!
Whitebear Whittington! Turn to me!

And early in the morning that other woman came, said, "Get on out now. Your time is up."

Well, the next evening the father of that woman called the young man just before bedtime. Said he wanted to have a word with him. So they walked out a ways and the old man said to him, says, "I couldn't sleep a bit the last two nights. There's some kind of a cryin' noise been goin' on in your room, and somebody singin' a mournful song right on up through the night."

The young man said he had slept uncommon sound the last two nights, hadn't heard a thing.

"Well now," says the old man, "I want you to be sure to stay awake tonight and listen and see what all that carryin' on is."

So that night the girl came and cracked the gold walnut and a big loom came out of it—just r'ared up in the house when she broke the nut. It was warped with gold warp and all you had to do was feed it bobbins of that gold thread and it wove right on—all by itself. The woman she heard it a-beatin' and she came running.

"Oh my! I must have that! What'll you take for your loom?"

The girl told her.

"Well!" she says, real hateful-like, "You can stay with him tonight but I'll tell ye right now it's the last time."

So she made the girl go out and then she looked about that sleepy pillow bein' still on the bed, went and fixed that sleepy dram, made it real strong, and when the young man came in to go to bed she handed it to him, made him drink it; but he kept it in his mouth and when she left he spit it out. Then he looked at that pillow and threw it off the bed. Laid down and closed his eyes. The woman she looked in at him to make sure he was asleep, then she let that girl in. She came in the room and saw him there with his eyes shut and her grief nearly killed her. She didn't know what she'd do. She came and sat on the edge of the bed and put her hand on his shoulder and started cryin':

> *Three drops of blood I've shed for thee!*
> *Three little babes I've born for thee!*
> *Whitebear Whittington! Turn to me!*

Well, time she called his name he opened his eyes and turned on her, and then he knew her. So he put his arms around her, and they went on to sleep.

The next morning that other woman came and found the door locked and she was mad as time. After they got up, the young man he came and called that woman's father, said, "Let's step outside. I want a word with *you*."

So they went out and he told the man, says, "If you had a lock and a key, and the key fitted the lock perfect, and you lost that key and got a new one, then you found the old key again, and it fitted the lock much better than the new one—which key would you keep?"

The old man answered him, says, "Why, I'd keep the old one."

"Well," says the young man, "I found my old wife last night and she suits me a lot better than your daughter does, so you can just have her back."

So they left and got their three children and went on home, and that spell on him was broke so he never was a bear again, and they lived happy.

COMMENT: This Kentucky variant has bits of "Cupid and Psyche," "East of the Sun and West of the Moon," "Beauty and the Beast," "The Small-Tooth Dog," and "The Black Bull of Norroway" (especially the chants), but like the other Grandfather Tales collected by Richard Chase in the Appalachians, it is melted down with a strong Pine Mountain flavor of its own. A great many English, Celtic, and European stories were preserved in isolated mountain areas where storytelling was a major source of entertainment, education, and social tradition.

The Three Daughters of King O'Hara

Irish

*T*here was a king in Desmond whose name was Coluath O'Hara, and he had three daughters. On a time when the king was away from home, the eldest daughter took a thought that she'd like to be married. So she went up in the castle, put on the cloak of darkness her father had, and wished for the most beautiful man under the sun as a husband for herself.

She got her wish. For scarcely had she put off the cloak of darkness when there came, in a golden coach with four horses, two black and two white, the finest man she had ever laid eyes on, who took her away.

When the second daughter saw what had happened to her sister, she put on the cloak of darkness and wished for the next best man in the world as a husband.

She put off the cloak, and straightaway there came, in a golden coach with four black horses, a man nearly as good as the first, who took her away.

The third sister put on the cloak and wished for the best white dog in the world.

Presently he came, with one man attending, in a golden coach and four snow-white horses, and took the youngest sister away.

When the king came home, the stable boy told him what had happened while he was gone. He was enraged beyond measure when he heard that his youngest daughter had wished for a white dog and had gone off with him.

When the first man brought his wife home he asked, "In what form will you have me in the daytime—as I am now in the daytime, or as I am now at night?"

"As you are now in the daytime."

So the first sister had her husband as a man in the daytime; but at night he was a seal.

The second man put the same question to the middle sister and got the same answer; so the second sister had her husband in the same form as the first.

When the third sister came to where the white dog lived, he asked her, "How will you have me to be in the daytime—as I am now in the day, or as I am now at night?"

"As you are now in the day."

So the white dog was a dog in the daytime, but the most beautiful of men at night.

After a time the third sister had a son, and one day, when her husband was going out to hunt, he warned her that if anything should happen to the child, not to shed a tear on that account.

While he was gone, a great gray crow that used to haunt the place came and carried the child away when it was a week old.

Remembering the warning, she shed not a tear for the loss.

All went on as before till another son was born. The husband used to go hunting every day, and again he said she must not shed a tear if anything happened.

When the child was a week old a great gray crow came and bore him away; but the mother did not cry or drop a tear.

All went well till a daughter was born. When she was a week old a great gray crow came and swept her away. This time the mother dropped one tear on a handkerchief, which she took out of her pocket, and then put back again.

When the husband came home from hunting and heard what the crow had done, he asked the wife, "Have you shed tears this time?"

"I have dropped one tear," she said.

Then he was very angry, for he knew what harm she had done by dropping that one tear.

Soon after their father invited the three sisters to visit him and be present at a great feast in their honor. They sent messages, each from her own palace, that they would come.

The king was very glad at the prospect of seeing his children, but the queen was grieved and thought it a great disgrace that her youngest daughter had no one to come home with her but a white dog.

The white dog was in dread that the king wouldn't leave him inside with the company, but would drive him from the castle to the yard and that the dogs outside wouldn't leave a patch of skin on his back, but would tear the life out of him.

The youngest daughter comforted him. "There is no danger to you," said she, "for wherever I am, you'll be, and wherever you go, I'll follow and take care of you."

When all was ready for the feast at the castle, and the company were assembled, the king was for banishing the white dog, but the youngest daughter would not listen to her father—would not let the white dog out of her sight, but kept him near her at the feast and divided with him the food that came to her.

When the feast was over, and all the guests had gone, the three sisters went to their own rooms in the castle.

Late in the evening the queen took the cook with her and stole in to see what was in her daughters' rooms. They were all asleep at the time. What should she see by the side of her youngest daughter but the most beautiful man she had ever laid eyes on.

Then she went to where the other two daughters were sleeping. There, instead of the two men who brought them to the feast, were two seals, fast asleep.

The queen was greatly troubled at the sight of the seals. When she and the cook were returning, they came upon the skin of the white dog. She caught it up as she went and threw it into the kitchen fire.

The Three Daughters of King O'Hara

The skin was not five minutes in the fire when it gave a crack that woke not only all in the castle, but all in the country for miles around.

The husband of the youngest daughter sprang up. He was very angry and very sorry and said, "If I had been able to spend three nights with you under your father's roof, I should have got back my own form again for good and could have been a man both in the day and the night; but now I must go."

He rose from the bed, ran out of the castle, and away he went as fast as ever his two legs could carry him, overtaking the one before him, and leaving the one behind. He was this way all that night and the next day. But he couldn't leave the wife, for she followed from the castle, was after him in the night and the day too, and never lost sight of him.

In the afternoon he turned and told her to go back to her father, but she would not listen to him. At nightfall they came to the first house they had seen since leaving the castle. He turned and said, "You go inside and stay in this house till morning. I'll pass the night outside where I am."

The wife went in. The woman of the house rose up, gave her a pleasant welcome, and put a good supper before her. She was not long in the house when a little boy came to her knee and called her "Mother."

The woman of the house told the child to go back to his place and not to come out again.

"Here are a pair of scissors," said the woman of the house to the king's daughter, "and they will serve you well. Whatever ragged people you see, if you cut a piece off their rags, that moment they will have new clothes of cloth of gold."

She stayed that night, for she had good welcome. Next morning when she went out, her husband said, "You'd better go home now to your father."

"I'll not go to my father if I have to leave you," said she.

So he went on, and she followed. It was that way all the day till night came. At night-fall they saw another house at the foot of a hill, and again the husband stopped and said, "You go in; I'll stop outside till morning."

The woman of the house gave her a good welcome. After she had eaten and drunk, a little boy came out of another room, ran to her knee, and said, "Mother." The woman of the house sent the boy back to where he had come from and told him to stay there.

Next morning, when the princess was going out to her husband, the woman of the house gave her a comb and said, "If you meet any person with a diseased and a sore head, and draw this comb over it three times, the head will be well and covered with the most beautiful golden hair ever seen."

She took the comb and went out to her husband.

"Leave me now," said he, "and go back to your own father."

"I will not," said she, "but I will follow you while I have the power." So they went forward that day, as on the other two.

At nightfall they came to a third house, at the foot of a hill, where the princess received a good welcome. After she had eaten supper, a little girl with only one eye came to her knee and said, "Mother."

The princess began to cry at sight of the child, thinking that she herself was the cause that she had but one eye. Then she put her hand into her pocket where she kept the handkerchief on which she had dropped the tear when the gray crow carried her infant away. She had never used the handkerchief since that day, for there was an eye on it.

She opened the handkerchief and put the eye in the girl's head. It grew into the socket that minute, and the child saw out of it as well as out of the other eye. Then the woman of the house sent the little one to bed.

Next morning, as the king's daughter was going out, the woman of the house gave her a whistle, and said, "Whenever you put this whistle to your mouth and blow on it, all the birds of the air will come to you from every quarter under the sun. Be careful of the whistle, as it may serve you greatly."

"Go back to your father's castle," said the husband when she came to him, "for I must leave you today."

They went on together a few hundred yards and then sat on a green hillock, and he told the wife, "Your mother has come between us; but for her we might have lived together all our days. If I had been allowed to pass three nights with you in your father's house, I should have got back my form of a man both in the daytime and the night. The Queen of Tir na n-Og [the land of youth] enchanted and put on me a spell, that unless I could spend three nights with a wife under her father's roof in Erin, I should bear the form of a white dog one half of my time. But if the skin of the dog should be burned before the three nights were over, I must go down to her kingdom and marry the queen herself. And it is to her I am going today. I have no power to stay, and I must leave you. So farewell, you'll never see me again on the upper earth."

He left her sitting on the mound, went a few steps forward to some bulrushes, pulled up one, and disappeared in the opening where the rush had been.

She stopped there, sitting on the mound lamenting, till evening, not knowing what to do. At last she bethought herself, and going to the rushes, pulled up a stalk, went down, followed her husband, and never stopped till she came to the lower land.

After a while she reached a small house near a splendid castle. She went into the house and asked if she could stay there till morning. "You can," said the woman of the house, "and welcome."

Next day the woman of the house was washing clothes, for that was how she made a living. The princess followed and helped her with the work. In the course of that day the Queen of Tir na n-Og and the husband of the princess were married.

Near the castle, and not far from the washerwoman's, lived a henwife with two ragged little daughters. One of them came around the washerwoman's house to play. The child looked so poor and her clothes were so torn and dirty that the princess took pity on her and cut the clothes with the scissors which she had.

That moment the most beautiful dress of cloth of gold ever seen on woman or child in that kingdom was on the henwife's daughter.

When she saw what she had on, the child ran home to her mother as fast as ever she could go.

"Who gave you that dress?" asked the henwife.

"A strange woman that is in that house beyond," said the little girl, pointing to the washerwoman's house.

The henwife went straight to the Queen of Tir na n-Og and said, "There is a strange woman in the place who will be likely to take your husband from you unless you banish her away or do something to her. For she has a pair of scissors different from anything ever seen or heard of in this country."

When the queen heard this she sent word to the princess that, unless the scissors were given up to her without delay, she would have the head off her.

The princess said she would give up the scissors if the queen would let her pass one night with her husband.

The queen answered that she was willing to give her the one night. The princess came and gave up the scissors and went to her own husband, but the queen had given him a drink, and he fell asleep and never woke till after the princess had gone in the morning.

Next day another daughter of the henwife went to the washerwoman's house to play. She was wretched looking, her head being covered with scabs and sores.

The princess drew the comb three times over the child's head, cured it, and covered it with beautiful golden hair. The little girl ran home and told her mother how the strange woman had drawn the comb over her head, cured it, and given her beautiful golden hair.

The henwife hurried off to the queen and said, "That strange woman has a comb with wonderful power to cure and give golden hair, and she'll take your husband from you unless you banish her or take her life."

The queen sent word to the princess that unless she gave up the comb, she would have her life.

The princess returned as answer that she would give up the comb if she might pass one night with the queen's husband.

The queen was willing, and gave her husband a draught as before. When the princess came, he was fast asleep and did not waken till after she had gone in the morning.

On the third day the washerwoman and the princess went out to talk, and the first daughter of the henwife went with them. When they were outside the town, the princess put the whistle to her mouth and blew. That moment the birds of the air flew to her from every direction in flocks. Among them was a bird of song and new tales.

The princess went to one side with the bird. "What means can I take," asked she, "against the queen to get back my husband? Is it best to kill her, and can I do it?"

"It is very hard," said the bird, "to kill her. There is no one in all Tir na n-Og who is able to take her life but her own husband. Inside a holly-tree in front of the castle is a wether [sheep], in the wether a duck, in the duck an egg, and in that egg is her heart and life. No man in Tir na n-Og can cut that holly-tree but her husband."

The princess blew the whistle again. A fox and a hawk came to her. She caught and put them into two boxes, which the washerwoman had with her, and took them to her new home.

When the henwife's daughter went home, she told her mother about the whistle. Away ran the henwife to the queen, and said, "That strange woman has a whistle that brings together all the birds of the air, and she'll have your husband yet, unless you take her head."

"I'll take the whistle from her, anyhow," said the queen. So she sent for the whistle.

The princess gave answer that she would give up the whistle if she might pass one night with the queen's husband.

The queen agreed and gave him a draught as on the other nights. He was asleep when the princess came and when she went away.

Before going, the princess left a letter with his servant for the queen's husband, in which she told how she had followed him to Tir na n-Og and had given the scissors, the comb, and the whistle to pass three nights in his company, but had not spoken to him because the queen had given him sleeping draughts, and that the life of the queen was in an egg, the egg in a duck, the duck in a wether, the wether in a holly-tree in front of the castle, and that no man could split the tree but he.

As soon as he got the letter the husband took an axe and went to the holly-tree. When he came to the tree he found the princess there before him, having the two boxes with the fox and the hawk in them.

He struck the tree a few blows. It split open, and out sprang the wether. He ran scarce twenty perches before the fox caught him. The fox tore him open; then the duck flew out. The duck had not flown fifteen perches when the hawk caught and killed her, smashing the egg. That instant the Queen of Tir na n-Og died.

The husband kissed and embraced his faithful wife. He gave a great feast, and when the feast was over, he burned the henwife with her house, built a palace for the washerwoman, and made his servant secretary.

They never left Tir na n-Og and are living there happily now; and so may we live here.

COMMENT: "The Three Daughters of King O'Hara" was published in *Myths and Folk-Lore of Ireland* (1889) by Jeremiah Curtin, whose Celtic collections contain several variants of the Cupid and Psyche tale type. Folklorists began collecting in Ireland while the oral tradition was still strong, and the archive in Dublin has shelves of handwritten volumes that contain tales in both Gaelic and English. Each story is carefully annotated with a record of the teller, the occasion upon which the story was told, the place and date of the telling, and sometimes a brief description of the audience response.

Black Bull of Norroway

Scottish

*I*n Norway, a long time ago, there lived a certain lady, and she had three daughters. The oldest of them said to her mother, "Mother, bake me a bannock [flat loaf of oat bread] and roast me a collop [slice of meat], for I'm going away to seek my fortune." Her mother did so; and the daughter went away to an old witch washerwife and told her purpose. The old wife bade her stay that day and look out of her back door and see what she could see. She saw nought the first day. The second day she did the same and saw nought. On the third day she looked again and saw a coach-and-sir coming along the road. She ran in and told the old wife what she saw. "Well," quoth the old woman, "yon's for you." So they took her into the coach and galloped off.

The second daughter next says to her mother, "Mother, bake me a bannock and roast me a collop, for I'm going away to seek my fortune." Her mother did so; and away she went to the old wife, as her sister had done. On the third day she looked out of the back door, and saw a coach-and-four coming along the road. "Well," quoth the old woman, "yon's for you." So they took her in, and off they set.

The third daughter says to her mother, "Mother, bake me a bannock and roast me a collop, for I'm going away to seek my fortune." Her mother did so; and away she went to the old witch. She bade her look out of her back door, and see what she could see. She did so; and when she came back said she saw nought. The third day she looked again, and on coming back said to the old wife she saw nought but a great Black Bull coming crooning along the road. "Well," quoth the old witch, "yon's for you." On hearing this she was next to distracted with grief and terror, but she was lifted up and set on his back, and away they went.

Aye they traveled, and on they traveled, till the lady grew faint with hunger. "Eat out of my right ear," says the Black Bull, "and drink out of my left ear, and set by your leaving." So she did as he said and was wonderfully refreshed. And long they rode and hard they rode, till they came in sight of a very big and bonny castle. "Yonder we must be this night," quoth the Bull, "for my elder brother lives yonder," and presently they were at the place. They lifted her off his back, took her in, and sent him away to a park for the night. In the morning, when they brought the Bull home, they took the lady into a fine shining parlor and gave her a beautiful apple, telling her not to break it till she was in the greatest strait ever a mortal was in in the world, and that would bring her out of it. Again she was lifted on the Bull's back, and after she had ridden far, and farther than I can tell, they came in sight of a far bonnier castle, far farther away than the last. Says the Bull to her, "Yonder we must be this night, for my second brother lives yonder," and they were at the place directly. They lifted her down, took her in, and sent the bull to the field for the night. In the morning they took the lady into a fine and rich room and gave her the finest pear she had ever seen, bidding her not to break it till she was in the greatest strait ever a mortal could be in, and that would get her out of it. Again she was lifted and set on his back, and away they went. And long they rode, and hard they rode, till they came in sight of the far biggest castle, and far farthest off, they had yet seen. "We must be yonder tonight," says the Bull, "for my young brother lives yonder," and they were there directly. They lifted her down, took her in, and sent the Bull to the field for the night. In the morning they took her into a room, the finest of all, and gave her a plum, telling her not to break it till she was in the greatest strait a mortal could be in, and that would get her out of it. Presently they brought home the Bull, set the lady on his back, and away they went.

And aye they rode, and on they rode, till they came to a dark and ugsome glen, where they stopped, and the lady lighted down. Says the Bull to her, "Here you must stay till I go and fight the Old One. You must seat yourself on that stone and move neither hand nor foot till I come back, else I'll never find you again. And if everything round about you turns blue, I have beaten the Old One; but should all things turn red, he'll have conquered me." She set herself down on the stone, and by-and-by all round her turned blue. Overcome with joy, she lifted one of her feet and crossed it over the other, so glad was she that her companion was victorious. The Bull returned and sought for her, but never could find her.

Long she sat, and aye she wept, till she wearied. At last she rose and went away, she didn't know where. On she wandered till she came to a great hill of glass that she tried all she could to climb, but wasn't able. Round the bottom of the hill she went, sobbing and seeking a passage over, till at last she came to a smith's house. The smith promised that if she would serve him seven years he would make her iron shoes, wherewith she could climb over the glassy hill. At seven years' end she got her iron shoes, climbed the glassy hill, and chanced to come to the old washerwife's habitation. There she was told of a gallant young knight that had given in some clothes all over blood to wash, and whoever washed them was to be his wife. The old wife had washed till she was tired, and then she set her daughter at it, and both washed, and they washed, and they washed, in hopes of getting the young knight; but for all they could do they couldn't bring out a stain. At length they set the stranger damsel to work, and whenever she began, the stains came out pure and clean, and the old wife made the knight believe it was her daughter had washed the clothes. So the knight and the eldest daughter were to be married, and the stranger damsel was distracted at the thought of it, for she was deeply in love with him. So she bethought her of her apple, and breaking it, found it filled with gold and precious jewelry, the richest she had ever seen. "All these," she said to the eldest daughter, "I will give you on condition that you put off your marriage for one day and allow me to go into his room alone at night." The lady consented, but meanwhile the old wife had prepared a sleeping drink and had given it to the knight, who drank it and never wakened till next morning. The live-long night the damsel sobbed and sang:

> Seven long years I served for thee,
> The glassy hill I climbed for thee,
> Thy bloody clothes I wrung for thee;
> And wilt thou not waken and turn to me?

Next day she knew not what to do for grief. Then she broke the pear and found it filled with jewelry far richer than the contents of the apple. With these jewels she bargained for permission to be a second night in the young knight's chamber. But the old wife gave him another sleeping drink, and again he slept till morning. All night she kept sighing and singing as before:

> Seven long years I served for thee,
> The glassy hill I climbed for thee,
> Thy bloody clothes I wrung for thee;
> And wilt thou not waken and turn to me?

Still he slept, and she nearly lost hope altogether. But that day, when he was out hunting, somebody asked him what noise and moaning was that they heard all last night in his bedchamber. He said, "I have heard no noise." But they assured him there was, and he resolved to keep awake that night to try to hear. That being the third night, and the damsel being between hope and despair, she broke her plum, and it held by far the richest jewelry of the three. She bargained as before, and the old wife, as before, took in the sleeping drink to the young knight's chamber, but he told her he couldn't drink it that night without sweetening. And when she went away for some honey to sweeten it with, he poured out the drink, and so made the old wife think he had drunk it. They all went to bed again, and the damsel began, as before, singing:

> Seven long years I served for thee,
> The glassy hill I climbed for thee,
> Thy bloody clothes I wrung for thee;
> And wilt thou not waken and turn to me?

He heard and turned to her. And she told him all that had befallen her, and he told her all that had happened to him. And he caused the old washerwife and her daughter to be burnt. And they were married, and he and she are living happy to this day, for aught I know.

COMMENT: This version of "The Black Bull of Norroway" is from *More English Fairy Tales* (1895) by famous British folklorist Joseph Jacobs, who adapted the tale from Robert Chambers' *Popular Rhymes, Fireside Stories, and Amusements of Scotland* (Edinburgh, 1842 and 1870). Other variants include "The Red Bull o' Norroway" and "The Brown Bear of Norway," which indicates a derivation from "East of the Sun and West of the Moon," in which the Beast is a bear.

Bull-of-all-the-Land

Jamaican

*T*here was a bull named King Henry and, in the day, Bull-of-all-the-Land. Well, in the day he put on bull clothes and the night he turned man. And one night the wife he lived with made up fire and burned the bull clothes, and after she burned the bull clothes, the man left the wife. Had three babies, and she told him to give her his clothes and she took her finger, prick, and dropped three drops of blood on the shirt front. And he went away, left them for three years.

And after he left them, she mashed three pairs of shoes to find him. And she walked till she caught a riverside, saw a washerwoman. And he said whoever would wash out the three drops of blood, he will marry her. Then the woman that was washing the shirt front said, "My lady, if you wash out the three drops of blood I will show you King Henry."

"Well then, only cut a lime and squeeze it upon the three drops of blood and wash it off!"

And the washerwoman left the woman at the riverside and ran up to King Henry, said, "I washed the blood!" And after she got up, he kept her in the yard, sent off for a minister, said in three days to marry the woman that washed out the blood.

In the night, they put the strange lady into a room close against King Henry, but the woman didn't know the king was there. And this woman that said she washed out the blood, gave him laudanum in tea and he dropped asleep. Then when the minister came, he heard the woman singing two nights; and he talked to King Henry, said what the woman was singing to him at night. And said what he drank in his tea. Nobody in the district knew his name was Bull-of-all-the-Land, only this woman; all others knew him as King Henry. Well the next night, sang again.

> *Return to me! Return to me, return to me, me bull of all the land.*
> *Return to me King Henry, return to me!*
> *I have three drops of blood, I washed for you.*
> *Return to me. Return to me, I have three drops of blood, I have washed for you.*
> *Return to me, King Henry,*
> *Return to me, return to me, me bull of all the land.*

As King Henry heard the singing, jumped right up. And the next day, married the woman, made her a lady. For nobody else knew he was Bull-of-all-the-Land.

COMMENT: Reprinted from Martha Warren Beckwith's *Jamaica Anansi Stories*, which the American Folk-Lore Society published in 1924, this sharply abbreviated version of "The Black Bull of Norroway" has a richly melodic dialect well matched to the accompanying music. For clarity, however, I have standardized the phonetic spellings and some of the grammar (*An' one night de wif him lib wid med up fire and bu'n de bull clo'es, an' after she bu'n de bull clo'es, de man lef' de wif* becomes *And one night the wife he lived with made up fire and burned the bull clothes, and after she burned the bull clothes, the man left the wife*); otherwise, it stands as it was recorded.

Prince White Hog

Missouri French

*I*t's good to tell that once upon a time there were an old man and an old woman. They had only one son, and they were poor. When the boy grew up and had his twenty-first birthday, he said to his father, "Papa, I'm going to go out and try to get a job, to make some money." His parents didn't want him to go and said to him, "We've done all right up till now. We can keep on the same way." But they couldn't persuade him. He said good-bye and left.

He had been traveling for two or three days and hadn't seen anything on the road or met anyone. But, finally, one day he met an old fairy. She said to him, "Good morning, my son," and he answered politely, "Good morning, Grandmother." Now he was on a good path and could walk along quickly. But she was on a path that was littered with logs and all sorts of brush, and it was hard for her to go forward. She said to him, "My son, would you be willing to change paths with me?" He answered, "Where are you going, Grandmother, I'll change paths with you. I'm young," he said. So then, he was on a bad path and couldn't go forward at all. He had to climb over rocks and logs and all sorts of obstacles. He kept going until finally he got back in the good path again. "Well!" he said. "Here's the good path again. Maybe now I'll be able to make some progress." He had traveled hardly any time at all when he met another old woman. "Good day, my son," she said. "Good day, Grandmother," he answered politely. "You're old to be out on the road like this." She said, "Yes, I'm pretty old, but I don't have a good path. Would you be willing to change paths with me, my son?" "I've already traded paths once," he answered, "and I found myself in a path that was blocked, and I have a long distance to go, too. Where are you going, Grandmother?" "I'm going to Paris," she answered. "Well," he said, "Since you're so old, I'll change paths with you, too. You're too old to be traveling on such rough paths."

So he traded paths with her and once again found himself on a terrible path. He said, "Well, I'm not trading paths anymore, old or not. I have a long way to go, and this is terrible. I can't get ahead at all. There's nothing but logs, rocks, stones, and all kinds of things that I have to climb over. If I ever find the right path, I'm not changing anymore with anyone." He kept on walking until he found the good path again. Then he said, "Old women can come along if they want to! I'm on the good path now, and I'm not giving it up again!"

So he started walking along the good path, and after a short time, he met another old fairy. She said, "Good day, my son." "Good day, Grandmother," he answered politely. "You're old to be walking along the road like this." "Yes," she answered, "I'm pretty old, and I have a long way to go." "Where are you going, Grandmother?" he asked. "I'm on my way to Paris," she answered. "My path is hard, and I'm not getting very far. Would you be willing to change paths with me?" "Well," he said, "I've already changed paths twice, and I have a long way to go, too. I said that I wouldn't change paths any more with anyone." "So, you don't want to trade paths with me, my son?" she asked.

"No," he answered, "I don't want to trade with anyone any more, Grandmother." The fairy then said to him, "Well, I'm putting a spell on you. You will be a hog by day, and by night you will be the most beautiful prince anyone has ever seen."

So, there he was in the woods, changed into Prince White Hog. But at night he turned into the most handsome prince the world had ever seen. He traveled along through the woods, toward his own house. He arrived at his own house, but no one recognized him. One night, he heard his father calling the hogs. He went where his father was feeding the other hogs. "Come and see!" the father called to his wife. "There's this beautiful white hog with the others." The old woman came and looked, and said, "That's the handsomest hog I've ever seen." Then the hog  said, "Yes, a handsome hog. He could even be your son." The father said, "What? Is that you, my son, turned into a hog?" "Yes, it's me," answered the hog. The father answered, "Well, I don't know what we're going to do with you, for sure. We'll have to build a stone pen and put you into it."

So the old man built a stone pen for his son and put him into it. Every day, he went out there to feed him. But one morning he went out, and he found the stone pen knocked down. "What in the world have you done?" asked the father. "You've knocked down your whole pen!" "Don't get upset," answered Prince White Hog. "I'm desperate to get married." "But who would want to marry a hog?" his father asked. "Well, you'll have to try to find me a wife," said Prince White Hog. The father went in and told his wife what had happened. She said, "But who would want to marry a hog?" He thought for a moment and said, "Well, my Aunt Blanche has three daughters. Maybe one of them would marry him." "You don't think Aunt Blanche would let one of her daughters marry a hog, do you?" asked the old woman. But the father just said, "I'll go and see."

So he left to go see. When he got there, he called out, "Hello!" and the old woman came out. "Hello, my son," she said. "Good morning, Aunt," answered Prince White Hog's father. "Come on in," said the old woman. "No, I came on business," he answered. "Prince White Hog badly wants a wife this morning. I came to find a wife for him. You don't think one of your daughters would want to marry him, do you?" The

Aunt answered, "Who in the world would want to marry a hog?" But her oldest daughter said, "It doesn't matter if he's a hog. I'll go." Her mother said, "Sure! I can just see you married to a hog." But the girl answered, "I'm going, and you can't stop me!" So she got ready and left with Prince White Hog's father.

When they got back they had a big wedding feast, and the girl married Prince White Hog. After the dinner, he went out and rooted all around in the mud. His nose got dirty, and then he took it into his head to come and kiss his new wife. She shouted at him, "Go away! Your nose is dirty!" So Prince White Hog turned away and went back out rooting in the mud. That evening, the old man said to the new bride, "Now, you have to go out in his pen and spend the night there with him. That's where he lives." But Prince White Hog was angry with her for turning him away, and he jumped on her and ate her up.

The next morning, the old man came out to bring them their breakfast. He went into the pen and looked around for his son's wife. He looked everywhere he could and then asked, "Where's your wife?" Prince White Hog answered, "Oh, I ate her!" "Well, you can well be crazy over women, but if you're going to eat them up like that, I can't imagine who else would want to marry you!" said the father. Things went on for quite a while, and the father fed his son every morning. Then one morning, he went out and found the pen knocked down again. He asked his son, "Why in the world did you do that? Your whole pen is knocked down!" "Don't ask!" answered Prince White Hog. "I need to get married again this morning." The father said, "Well, I don't know who will marry you, since you eat up your wives as you do."

But he went back in the house, told his wife about it, and said, "Aunt Blanche still has two daughters. I guess I might as well go and see her." So he went and when he got there, he called out, "Hello!" The old woman came out and invited him in. He said, "No, I can't stay. I'm in a hurry. I came on business. Prince White Hog wants to get married again this morning, and I'm looking for a wife for him. You don't think one of your daughters would want to come, do you?" "Well," she answered, "they'd have to be crazy to go and marry him, just to get themselves eaten up. But the older of her two remaining daughters said, "I'll go!" Her mother answered, "Well, if you're silly enough to go and get eaten up like your sister, go ahead." So the girl got ready and left with the old man. When they got back, she got married to Prince White Hog and had another big wedding feast. After they had eaten, Prince White Hog went out rooting in the mud, got his nose good and dirty, and then decided to come in and kiss his wife. He went up to her and put his feet on her knees to kiss her. "Get out of here with your dirty nose!" she

Prince White Hog

screamed at him. She slapped him and made him leave. So, he turned around and went back out and rooted around until night came. When it got dark, the old man told the new bride that she would have to go out and spend the night with Prince White Hog in the stone pen, because that was where he lived. But that night, Prince White Hog was angry with his bride. He jumped on her and ate her up.

The next morning, the old man went out to give them their breakfast. He started looking for the young woman, but he couldn't find her. He asked, "Where did your wife go?" Prince White Hog answered, "Well, I ate her." The father said to him, "Well, if you go on eating all your wives like that, you don't really want a wife!" But Prince White Hog answered, "As long as they're going to treat me like that, slapping me in the face and calling me 'Dirty-Nose' when I go to kiss them, I'm going to eat them." Things went smoothly for a while, and then one morning again the father went out to feed his son and found the stone pen all knocked down. The father said, "Why in the world did you do this? Your stone pen is all knocked down again!" Prince White Hog told him, "Don't ask! I want to get married again this morning." The father said, "I don't know where you're going to find a wife, since you eat them all up."

But he came into the house and told his wife that Prince White Hog wanted to get married again. She said, "Well I surely don't know where you're going to find him a wife this time." The old man said, "Well, Aunt Blanche still has one daughter left. I'll go and see her. You never know. She might want to do it." He left to go see his Aunt Blanche, and when he got there, he cried out, "Hello!" The old woman came out and said, "Good day, my son. Come on in and visit." He said, "No, Aunt, I don't have time. I'm in a hurry. I came on business. Prince White Hog really wants to get married this morning, and I'm looking for a wife for him. You don't think that your daughter would marry him, do you?" "Well, I don't know what she would be thinking," answered the old woman, "to marry a hog, especially one who eats all his wives." But her one remaining daughter said to her, "I want to go Mama." "No, you won't go," answered her mother. "Yes, I am going," she answered.

So, she left with Prince White Hog's father, and they had another big wedding feast. After they had eaten, Prince White Hog did the same thing: he went out rooting in the dirt and got his nose all muddy. Then, he took it into his head to come in and kiss his wife. He came, jumped up into her lap, and put his paws on her. She grabbed him around the neck and kissed him. She caressed him for a while, and then he turned around and went out to root until evening. That evening, the old man said to his new daughter-in-law, "Well, now you'll have to go out and spend the night in the stone pen with him. That's where he lives."

They sat up together until nine o'clock, and then Prince White Hog turned into the most handsome prince the world has ever seen. She was as happy as she could be when she saw this handsome prince with her. But he told her, "You mustn't tell anyone at all about this. If you do tell someone, you will have to wear out a pair of steel shoes and a steel dress before you would find me again." One day, he said to her, "Aren't you a little lonely for your mother? You can go and visit her as much as you would like." So one morning, she said to him, "I think I will go and visit my mother." "Go ahead," he said. So, she left to go to her mother's house. When she got there, her mother sent for her aunt to have lunch with them. But after they had eaten, at about four o'clock in the afternoon, the girl said, "Now, it's time for me to go back home." "Is it possible that you would go back to eat dinner with a hog?" asked her mother. They laughed at her and got her angry, and she said, "Yes! He's a hog during the day, but at night he turns into the most handsome prince you've ever laid eyes on."

So Prince White Hog was found out. When the girl thought about what she had said, she ran toward her house as fast as she could. When she got there, she looked everywhere for Prince White Hog and called and called, but she saw that he was gone. She thought of what he had said: before she could find him again she had to wear out a steel dress and a pair of steel shoes.

So she went to the blacksmith and had him make her a steel dress and a pair of steel shoes, and then she set out traveling. The first evening, she came to the house of an old fairy. The fairy said to her, "I know what you're looking for. If I didn't know so well, I'd eat you up. Your dress isn't very worn yet. Let me see the soles of your shoes. Hm! They're hardly used at all either. You still have a long way to go!" She said, "You're going to stay here with me tonight. But then tomorrow, with my power, you'll go a lot farther, and you'll be able to put a lot of wear on your shoes and your dress."

So the next morning, the girl set out again. She walked all day long, and that evening she came to the house of another fairy. This fairy said to her, "Well, if I didn't know what you are looking for, I'd bite you in two like a grain of salt! Show me your shoes. Your dress isn't too worn out yet." The girl showed her shoes to the old woman. They were getting pretty worn down. "Come on in and spend the night here with me," the old woman said to her. "By my power, your dress and your shoes will be pretty worn out when you get to where you're going tomorrow evening." So the girl stayed the second night with the old woman.

When the time came for her to leave the next morning, the old woman said to her, "By my power, you'll get there tonight. Prince White Hog is staying with a king and is getting ready to get married. I'm going to give you a magic wand. When you get to that king's castle, hire on as a cook. Whatever you have to make, just tap the table with your wand and wish for the best dinner or supper they've ever had there, and you will have it." Then the old woman gave the girl a beautiful silk handkerchief. It shone like gold. She said, "The Princess who is going to marry him will want this. There will be a little boy whom that Princess is using as a spy. He'll see everything you do and will tell the Princess about it. She'll send him to you to see if you want to sell her the handkerchief. You are to tell him that you won't sell it, lend it, or give it. She has to earn it. Tell her that if she lets you sleep with the prince that night, she can have it. She'll tell you that you can sleep with him just for that night. You will be able to talk to Prince White Hog and let him know that you're his wife and maybe get him back.

Just as the old woman had said, the little boy saw the beautiful silk handerkerchief that the girl had. He went and told the Princess that the cook had this beautiful silk handkerchief that shone like gold. She sent him to ask the girl if she would sell it. The little boy went running and said to the girl, "The Princess told me to ask you if you would like to sell that handkerchief." The cook answered, "I won't sell that little handkerchief, or lend it, or give it away. But she can earn it." The little boy ran back to the Princess to tell her what the cook had said. The Princess sent him back to the cook to find out what she would have to do earn the handkerchief.

The little boy came back and asked the cook what would have to be done to win the handkerchief. The cook answered, "If she lets me sleep with the prince tonight, I'll let her have the handkerchief." So that night, the Princess, to get the handkerchief, said to the prince, "You're going to have to sleep with the cook tonight." That night, the cook went in and got ready to sleep with the prince. But the Princess fixed up a cup of opium and said to the little boy, "Bring this to the prince and tell him to drink it so that he'll sleep well." The little boy brought in the drink, and the prince drank it up. No sooner had he drunk the mixture than he fell into a deep sleep. The cook waited for a while, and then finally she started poking and pulling the prince so that she could tell him her story. But she was never able to wake him up.

The next morning, she got up early and went out to make their breakfast. At noon, everyone came in to eat the dinner that the cook had made. The king was proud of her work and boasted about what a good cook she was. Then in the afternoon, the old fairy gave her a golden ball. She began to play with it, throwing it up in the air and catching it. The little boy who was playing spy was still there, and he went to tell the Princess about the beautiful golden ball that the cook was playing with. He said, "You should see that pretty ball that the cook has. It's the most beautiful thing I've ever seen!" The Princess said to him, "Go ask the cook if she would be willing to sell it to me." The little boy ran to the cook and asked her, but the cook said to him, "This ball is not to sell, or to lend, or to give. It has to be earned." The Princess told the little boy to ask the cook what would have to be done to earn the golden ball. The little boy went running back to the cook to ask her, and she said to him, "Tell the Princess that if she lets me sleep with the prince again tonight, she can have the golden ball." The Princess sent the boy back to the cook to tell her that she could sleep with the prince just one more time, but that she wouldn't sleep with him again after that! The cook gave the ball to the little boy, and he brought it to the Princess.

When nighttime came, the Princess said to Prince White Hog, "You'll have to sleep with the cook again tonight." "That's fine," he said. But when the time came for them to go to bed, the Princess fixed another glass of opium and sent it to the prince with the little boy. She said, "Here, bring this to the prince and tell him to drink it so that he'll sleep well." No sooner had the prince drunk the mixture than he fell sound asleep. The cook waited awhile. When she thought that everyone in the house must be asleep, she began to talk to him.

The little boy, after he had given the glass of opium to the prince, had hidden himself behind the door. He hadn't gone to bed. The cook began to poke Prince White Hog when he didn't answer. "Are you asleep?" she asked. "Don't you want to talk to me? What's the matter?" she said. "I have only one more night that I can sleep with you, and then, the day after tomorrow, my blood will be shed. You know what you told me, that I would have to wear out a pair of steel shoes and steel dress in order to find you again. Well, I wore them both out, and now you don't want to talk to me!"

The little boy hidden behind the door was listening and heard everything that she said. When she was quiet, the little boy left and went to his own bed. The next morning, the cook got up and made breakfast for everyone. At noon she made dinner. After they had all eaten dinner, Prince White Hog said to the Princess, "I'm going to go out and take a nap by the spring, in the shade." The little boy followed him out to talk to him. Prince White Hog wanted the little boy to go away, but he said, "I've got to tell you something. I've got to tell you what the cook was saying to you last night." Then Prince White Hog got up and listened to the little boy. The prince asked, "Well, what was she saying?" The boy answered, "She said that she could only sleep with you one more night and then her blood would be shed. She said that she'd used up a pair of steel shoes and now you didn't want to talk to her." Prince White Hog said to the little boy then, "Go back to the house and don't say a word about this to anyone, do you hear?"

So the little boy went back to the house, looked through the door, and saw that the cook was playing with a pretty gold ring. He went to tell the Princess about it, and she said, "Go and ask her if she would be willing to sell it to me." He ran to the cook and said, "Would you be willing to sell that pretty gold ring to the Princess?" The cook said, "Tell the Princess that this gold ring is not to be sold, or lent, or given. It has to be earned." The Princess sent him back to the cook to ask how it could be earned.

The little boy came back and asked the cook what would have to be done to earn the ring. She said to him, "Tell the Princess that if she lets me sleep with him just this one more time, she can have it." The Princess said, "Well, tell her that she can sleep with him just this one more time. But she can't do it anymore after tonight, because tomorrow is our wedding day." He told this to the cook, and she sent him back to the Princess with the ring.

So, after supper, everyone stayed up until about nine o'clock. At nine o'clock, the Princess told the prince that he would have to sleep with the cook just one more time, but that the next day they would be married. When the prince was getting ready to go to bed, the Princess fixed another glass of opium and sent it in with the little boy. "Here," she said to the boy, "tell the prince to drink this so that he will sleep well." The little boy went in with the drink. The prince took the glass, turned around, and emptied it out behind the bed. When the cook thought that everyone must be asleep in the house, she nudged the prince. "Are you asleep?" she asked. No, he wasn't asleep. The cook asked him, "How come you didn't want to talk to me the other nights when we've slept together?" "Well those drinks they were giving me were putting me to sleep," he told her. Then the cook said, "You remember, you told me that I'd have to wear out a pair of steel shoes and a steel dress before I could find you again?" The prince said, "Don't say any more. Tomorrow, we'll be together again."

The next day, the cook made the wedding feast. With her magic wand, she wished for the best dinner that they had ever had in that house. They were going to get married in the afternoon. When dinner was ready, she told them to come and eat. The king said, "I'd like nothing better than to tell stories before dinner." Everyone said to the old king, "Well, tell yours first, since you're the oldest!" So the old king told his story. Then it was the prince's turn. He said, "If someone brought you a big herd of horses and let you pick one out, and then told you that you could keep the one you had picked, what would you think if they didn't want to give you the one you wanted?" The king said, "That's just like me. If I picked one, I would want to have my first choice. I wouldn't want to let it go."

"Well," said the prince, "that's just like me, too. I would want to have my first choice. I was going to marry your daughter. But that cook is my first wife. She had lost me because she had betrayed me, and she had to wear out a pair of steel shoes and a steel dress before she could find me again. But she's my wife and my first choice. Today, she has found me again. I would like to go back with her." The king said, "Yes, you're right. If she's your wife, you should go back with her." They sent me here to tell you the story. I was all ready to have dinner with them, but they wouldn't let me stay there long enough.

COMMENT: "It's good to tell you" is the traditional opening formula for Missouri French folktales, which were written down in dialect by Joseph Carrière and published in 1937. The young man in this tale, enchanted into the shape of a hog by an old fairy for whom he refuses to do a favor, doesn't show much patience with the first two wives who spurn him—he eats them both. But the third girl keeps her word, transforms him, and then has to wear out a steel dress, along with the traditional pair of steel shoes, to get him back after betraying his secret to her mother.

The Enchanted Prince

Spanish American

*O*nce there was a woman who had nine daughters. The oldest had nine eyes, the next had eight eyes, the next seven eyes, the next six eyes, the next five, the next four, the next three, the next one eye, and the youngest two eyes.

One day the daughters went out for a walk through a forest and the youngest one, the one who had two eyes, left the others and met a beautiful green bird, and he asked her to marry him. He told her that he was an enchanted prince and that if she did as he asked, she would someday be a queen. Two Eyes promised to marry him and agreed to do what he asked. Green Bird then flew away.

Two Eyes then went to her sisters and told them all about her meeting with the bird. They immediately began to make fun of her. "What are you going to do with a bird?" they asked her. "He will take you away to a nest somewhere." "It is my wish," she replied. "I am going to marry him even if he is a bird." And from there they went home to tell their mother.

Soon the bird arrived to ask for Two Eyes in marriage. The mother and the sisters objected. But Two Eyes insisted and finally went away with the bird and married him. Green Bird took her to the mountains to a beautiful palace. He gave his bride the keys to all the rooms of the palace. He told her again that he was an enchanted prince, to be very careful, and not say a word about the enchantment. He furthermore told her that the palace had nine windows and that he would be with her only during the night. He would fly away in the morning and come to sing at each one of the nine windows at nine o'clock and then remain. He then gave her a little bottle of sleeping water and told her to put some on the sheets of the bed so that anyone sleeping on it would go to sleep and would not see him or hear him sing. The bird then flew away for the first time.

The mother of the daughters became envious and called Nine Eyes and said to her, "You must go now to see your sister in order to find out who the bird is. You have nine eyes and you can see more than your sisters." Nine Eyes left immediately.

When she arrived at her sister's beautiful palace, Two Eyes went out to meet her, took her inside, and showed her the nine windows of the palace. "But I don't see your husband, Green Bird, anywhere," she said. Two Eyes did not say anything in reply. Finally Nine Eyes got tired of seeing all the things the palace contained and she said she wished to go to bed. Two Eyes took her to a bed, and secretly she put a few drops of the sleeping water on the sheets. Nine Eyes went to sleep immediately.

Green Bird arrived at nine o'clock as he had promised, sang beautifully before each of the nine windows of the palace, and Nine Eyes didn't see anything or hear anything. Then he entered the palace as a handsome prince. He asked his wife, "Who came?" "My sister, Nine Eyes," replied Two Eyes. "Well and good," said the prince. "If there is no envy, everything is all right, but if there is envy and we get into trouble, I will leave and you will never see me again." Before dawn he left again, but he told his wife to give her sister anything she wished from the things she had in the palace.

In the morning Nine Eyes woke up and went to see her sister. She was surprised that she had seen nothing of the bird. She asked Two Eyes, but Two Eyes said nothing that would satisfy her. She remembered what her husband had told her and did not wish to betray him. Nine Eyes then went home laden with rich gifts, and she told her mother that she had not seen any bird at the palace.

The next night Eight Eyes was sent to the palace of Two Eyes. "Your sister who has nine eyes has not seen the bird," said the mother. "Now let us see whether you can see anything." She arrived at the palace and asked about the bird, but Two Eyes merely took her around and showed her all the palace, the nine windows, and everything else. She fell asleep also after Two Eyes put her to bed with sleeping water on the sheets. At nine o'clock Green Bird appeared again, sang at the nine windows, and again remained with his wife. Eight Eyes did not see or hear anything.

The same thing happened to Seven Eyes, to Six Eyes, to Five Eyes, to Four Eyes, and to Three Eyes. All did as Nine Eyes and Eight Eyes had done. Each one of them went to sleep and saw nothing. And each evening, when they were in the palace asleep, Green Bird arrived at nine o'clock, sang at each one of the nine windows, and remained all night with his wife without being seen by them. "Now we must be more careful than ever," the prince said to his wife. "If there is no envy, I shall soon be disenchanted and we will be king and queen."

One Eye then said to her mother and to her sisters, "I have only one eye, but I am going to show you that I can see more than all of you together."

The next morning, after Green Bird had flown away to the mountains, Two Eyes looked out of one of her windows and saw One Eye coming. "Well, there is my one-eyed sister coming to see me," she said. She awaited her gladly and as soon as she arrived, she went out to meet her. "How are you, sister?" said One Eye. "Very well, indeed," said Two Eyes. "You must let me show you the palace that Green Bird, my husband, gave me." "I am too tired," said One Eye. "I really don't care to see anything. Now that I have seen you, I think I had better go home." "Oh, no," said Two Eyes, "you must stay for dinner!" Finally she stayed. At night she went to bed also, but Two Eyes did not put the sleeping water on the sheets. "My little sister is so small and she is so tired. Surely she will not see anything," she said. When One Eye went to bed, she said to Two Eyes, "Cover me up with the sheet." When Two Eyes went away, she made a small hole in the sheet to look through.

At nine o'clock Green Bird arrived and sang at the nine windows, and One Eye saw and heard everything. She was covered with the sheet, but through the hole she saw with her one eye. When the bird sang at the last window, he became a handsome prince, as he did every evening, and One Eye saw everything.

"Good Evening, my love," said the prince to Two Eyes. "Who came this evening?" "My sister, my little sister," replied Two Eyes. "Yes, I know all about it," said the prince. "You have been ungrateful and unfaithful to me. Tomorrow you will see me leave in a carriage drawn by a black crow." Then he left, and she remained very sad.

"What did you see, little sister?" asked Two Eyes of One Eye late in the morning when she got up. "Nothing. I didn't see anything. Please give me my breakfast so that I can go home." Two Eyes gave her her breakfast, and she left. Then Two Eyes remained alone, abandoned by her sisters and by her husband.

As soon as One Eye reached home, she told her mother and her sisters all she had seen. "My sisters with so many eyes could not see anything, and I with just one eye have seen everything," she said. When the envious mother had heard everything, she said, "This evening I am going myself." And she did as she said. She went secretly and placed pieces of glass in all the windows so the bird would cut himself and die, and she and her daughters would come to possess the beautiful palace. As soon as she had done the mischief, she left.

The bird arrived at nine, as was his custom, and began to sing at the first window. He sang well there, but as he continued to sing at the other windows, his voice became weaker and weaker because he was all cut up with the broken glass the mother of Two Eyes had placed on the windows. He entered his room very weak and said to Two Eyes, "What an ungrateful thing you have done! Now I must leave, as I told you. You will never see me again." A carriage appeared, drawn by a black crow, the wounded prince entered, and he soon disappeared.

Two Eyes almost died of grief. But she watched the direction the carriage had taken, and taking her royal garments and her little bottle of sleeping water with her, she departed in search of her husband. She traveled and traveled, and finally, almost exhausted, she sat down at the foot of a poplar to rest. Presently she heard some birds in the tree conversing. One bird was saying that the prince was very ill and that there was only one way he could be cured. "How can he be cured?" asked another bird. "By

The Enchanted Prince

killing us and taking the blood and anointing the wounds of the prince with it. In that way all the glass will come out, and he will get well."

When Two Eyes heard this, she emptied the sleeping water out of her little bottle. The little birds then went to sleep, and she killed them all and put their blood in the bottle. Then she went her way in search of the prince, her husband. She searched and searched, but could not find him.

Finally she went to see the moon. She asked the moon whether she had seen a sick prince anywhere. "I have been at every window of every house in the world and have not seen such a prince," said the moon. Then she went to see the sun. She asked the sun the same question. "Indeed I have seen him," replied the sun. "He is very ill at his father's house. I cannot take you there, but maybe the wind can take you." Two Eyes then went to see the wind. "Yes, indeed, I know that prince well," said the wind. "The king, his father, has brought doctors from all parts of the world, but none can cure him. If you wish, I can take you to where he is." Two Eyes thanked him and asked him to take her at once. "Get inside of this leather bag and take that knife with you," said the wind. "I will blow you over there, and as soon as you land, cut a hole in the bag and get out."

A great wind arose and took the bag to the house of the prince. When it was grounded, Two Eyes cut a hole through the leather and got out. She went to the door of the palace and asked the servants about the prince. "He is very ill," they said. "The doctors say he will surely die." Then she told them to tell the king that if they would allow her to go into the palace, she could cure the prince. The king said that she could come in. When she entered, the king told her, "If you can cure the prince, I will support you for the rest of your life." She asked for a sheet and put on it the blood of the birds that she had in the little bottle. Then she ordered that the prince should be wrapped in it so the blood would cover the wounds. This she did three times, and the pieces of glass began to come out from the wounds. And soon all the pieces came out, and the prince was completely cured. The king then built a house for Two Eyes and said he would fulfill his promise.

The prince, however, had forgotten his former bride and was about to be married to a beautiful princess. And Two Eyes knew everything and saw everything. And she had with her her dresses, her rings, and other presents that the prince had given her. When the day of the wedding arrived, the princess came to the palace of the prince because he was much richer. And when the ceremony was about to begin, Two Eyes went to her house and dressed herself in her queenly garments, with her rings and with her crown. When the prince entered the church with his new bride, Two Eyes suddenly appeared at his side also. The prince at once recognized her and said, "Here is my true wife!" And he left the new bride and went out with his wife.

And the envious mother and sisters found no palace at all. All they found was a deserted plain.

COMMENT: Part of a rich tradition of Spanish folklore collected in northern New Mexico and southern Colorado, this tale focuses on the envy of the heroine's mother, who sends her eight other daughters to spy on the bird husband and then tries to kill him. The imagery of the nine girls with their one to nine eyes, the nine windows at which the green bird perches to sing every night at nine, the broken glass that makes the bird bleed, and the other birds' blood that removes the pieces of glass show an uncommon and lyrical balance that's reflected in the poetic justice of the ending: those who covet all find nothing.

The Story of Five Heads

African

*T*here was a man living in a certain place who had two daughters big enough to be married.

One day the man went over the river to another village, which was the residence of a great chief. The people asked him to tell them the news. He replied that there was no news in the place that he came from. Then the man inquired about the news of their place. They said the news of their place was that the chief wanted a wife.

The man went home and said to his two daughters, "Which of you wishes to be the wife of a chief?"

The eldest replied, "I wish to be the wife of a chief, my father." The name of that girl was Mpunzikazi.

The man said, "At that village I visited, the chief wishes for a wife. You, my daughter, shall go."

The man called all his friends and assembled a large company to go with his daughter to the village of the chief. But the girl would not consent that those people should go with her.

She said, "I will go alone to be the wife of the chief."

Her father replied, "How can you, my daughter, say such a thing? Is it not so that when a girl goes to present herself to her husband she should be accompanied by others? Be not foolish, my daughter."

The girl still said, "I will go alone to be the wife of the chief."

Then the man allowed his daughter to do as she chose. She went alone, no bridal party accompanying her, to present herself at the village of the chief who wanted a wife.

As Mpunzikazi was in the path, she met a mouse.

The mouse said, "Shall I show you the way?"

The girl replied, "Just get away from before my eyes."

The mouse answered, "If you do like this, you will not succeed."

Then she met a frog.

The frog said, "Shall I show you the way?"

Mpunzikazi replied, "You are not worthy to speak to me, as I am to be the wife of a chief."

The frog said, "Go on then. You will see afterward what will happen."

When the girl got tired, she sat down under a tree to rest. A boy who was herding goats in that place came to her, he being very hungry.

The boy said, "Where are you going my eldest sister?"

Mpunzikazi replied in an angry voice, "Who are you that you should speak to me? Just get away from before me."

The boy said, "I am very hungry. Will you not give me of your food?"

She answered, "Get away quickly."

The boy said, "You will not return if you do this."

She went on her way again and met with an old woman sitting by a big stone.

The old woman said, "I will give you advice. You will meet with trees that will laugh at you: you must not laugh in return. You will see a bag of thick milk: you must not eat of it. You will meet a man whose head is under his arm: you must not take water from him."

Mpunzikazi answered, "You ugly thing! Who are you that you should advise me?"

The old woman continued in saying those words.

The girl went on. She came to a place where there were many trees. The trees laughed at her, and she laughed at them in return. She saw a bag of thick milk, and she ate of it. She met a man carrying his head under his arm, and she took water to drink from him.

She came to the river of the village of the chief. She saw a girl there dipping water from the river. The girl said, "Where are you going to, my sister?"

Mpunzikazi replied, "Who are you that you should call me sister? I am going to be the wife of a chief."

The girl drawing water was the sister of the chief. She said, "Wait, I will give you advice. Do not enter the village by this side."

Mpunzikazi did not stand to listen, but just went on.

She reached the village of the chief. The people asked her where she came from and what she wanted.

She answered, "I have come to be the wife of the chief."

They said, "Who ever saw a girl go without a retinue to be a bride?"

They said also, "The chief is not at home. You must prepare food for him, that when he comes in the evening he may eat."

They gave her millet to grind. She ground it very coarse and made bread that was not nice to eat.

In the evening she heard the sound of a great wind. That wind was the coming of the chief. He was a big snake with five heads and large eyes. Mpunzikazi was very much frightened when she saw him. He sat down before the door and told her to bring his food. She brought the bread which she had made. Makanda Mahlanu (Five Heads) was not satisfied with that bread. He said, "You shall not be my wife," and he struck her with his tail and killed her.

Afterward the sister of Mpunzikazi said to her father, "I also wish to be the wife of a chief."

Her father replied, "It is well, my daughter. It is right that you should wish to be a bride."

The man called all his friends, and a great retinue prepared to accompany the bride. The name of the girl was Mpunzanyana.

On the way they met a mouse.

The mouse said, "Shall I show you the road?"

Mpunzanyana replied, "If you will show me the way I shall be glad."

Then the mouse pointed the way.

She came into a valley, where she saw an old woman standing by a tree.

The old woman said to her, "You will come to a place where two paths branch off. You must take the little one, because if you take the big one you will not be fortunate."

Mpunzanyana replied, "I will take the little path, my mother." She went on.

Afterward she met a cony [rabbit].

The cony said, "The village of the chief is close by. You will meet a girl by the river: you must speak nicely to her. They will give you millet to grind: you must grind it well. When you see your husband, you must not be afraid."

She said: "I will do as you say, cony."

In the river she met the chief's sister carrying water.

The chief's sister said, "Where are you going?"

Mpunzanyana replied, "This is the end of my journey."

The chief's sister said, "What is the object of your coming to this place?"

Mpunzanyana replied, "I am with a bridal party."

The chief's sister said, "That is right, but will you not be afraid when you see your husband?"

Mpunzanyana answered, "I will not be afraid."

The chief's sister pointed out the hut in which she should stay. Food was given to the bridal party. The mother of the chief took millet and gave it to the bride, saying, "You must prepare food for your husband. He is not here now, but he will come in the evening."

In the evening she heard a very strong wind, which made the hut shake. The poles fell, but she did not run out. Then she saw the chief Makanda Mahlanu coming. He asked for food. Mpunzanyana took the bread she had made and gave it to him. He was very much pleased with that food and said,

"You shall be my wife." He gave her very many ornaments.
Afterwards Makanda Mahlanu became a man, and Mpunzanyana
continued to be the wife he loved best.

COMMENT: Published in an 1882 collection of "traditional tales current among the people living on the eastern border of the Cape colony" of South Africa, this story was adapted in John Steptoe's picture book, *Mufaro's Beautiful Daughters*, which was a Caldecott Honor Book in 1988. The contrasting behavior of the two questing sisters, whose tests form the backbone of the story, presents a moral behavior code that makes the chief's transformation seem like an afterthought.

The Ten Serpents

Israeli

*O*nce upon a time there was a poor orphan who was diligent and righteous. One night, in a dream, an old man appeared before him and put a diamond in his hand, saying, "With this diamond you will become rich, build a house, and wed. You will have but one daughter, whom you must guard carefully, because you will have to return her in exchange for the diamond. If you do not heed this warning, you will become poor once again." The old man finished his words and disappeared.

In the morning the boy awoke and found a huge diamond in his hand. He sold it, bought goods, and began to wander from town to town, carrying on trade.

Years passed, and the youth became a very rich merchant, the husband of a pretty wife, and the father of a beautiful daughter without match in all the kingdom.

One day, when the merchant was returning home, a serpent suddenly crept out of the forest. The merchant tried to make his escape, but it was as if his legs were stuck to the spot; he could not move. And the serpent crept nearer and nearer. Suddenly the merchant heard a voice from above, "Venerable sir! If you want to escape death, give me your daughter in marriage. If not, the serpent will bite you to death."

Remembering his dream and the warning of the old man, the merchant agreed, whereupon the snake vanished and the merchant found he could move once more. As he began walking away, he heard the mysterious voice again: "Venerable merchant, if you cheat me, you will die."

The merchant went home, and lo, his house, garden, and even his servants had disappeared. In their place stood a poor miserable hut. The merchant's wife and daughter were both poorly clad, and suddenly he noticed that his own clothes, too, were in tatters. Immediately he regretted what he had said to the mysterious voice, and he related to his family all that had happened to him. His sorrow was so great that he wished to die.

When his beautiful and obedient daughter saw her father's distress, she said, "I will fulfill your promise, father. I am willing to live a life of anguish so that you may be spared."

Weeks passed, months went by, and the merchant's family became used to their poverty. Then one night there was a knock at the door of the hut, and on opening it, the merchant beheld a huge and terrible serpent. It opened its mouth and said in a human voice, "I am the stranger to whom you promised your daughter."

The father turned to his daughter in anguish and said, "I prefer to die than to give you up in marriage to this terrible monster."

However, the obedient daughter sacrificed herself to marry the serpent in order to save her father's life. The snake gave her a ring as a token of betrothal, and they went to the second room and shut the door. Suddenly the serpent shook himself and shed his skin, and lo! A handsome youth stood in front of the daughter. He said to her, "If you want to live happily with me, do not ask any questions and do not tell anyone, even your parents, what you have seen. Every morning I will leave you, but I will return at nightfall."

You can well imagine that the daughter fell in love with this handsome young man at first sight and promised to carry out his bidding.

In the morning the daughter awoke to find that the serpent was no longer there. In the meantime her parents, who had not slept a wink the whole night, were full of fear and anxiety for their daughter. They did not believe their eyes when they saw her leaving the room, safe and sound, in fact, joyous and happy. They began to shower her with questions, but their daughter, who had always respected them, refused to answer.

A few days passed, and the parents began to rebuke their daughter for hiding the truth from them who loved her so dearly. At last the daughter broke down and disclosed the secret. That evening the serpent appeared but did not shed his skin as usual. He said in a sad voice, "As you have broken your promise, I shall have to leave you. Do not search for me anywhere because you will not find me."

The daughter did not even have time to apologize; in the winking of an eye, the serpent had vanished. The daughter became very sad. She would lock herself everyday in her room, refusing to admit anyone.

Nearby lived a poor family. It so happened that one day their daughter was playing in the street with her doll. A dog passed by, seized the doll, and scampered off. The child followed him. The dog went beyond the town, and the child still trailed behind him. There was always the same distance between them.

Suddenly a fox jumped out of the bushes and chased the dog. The dog became frightened, dropped the doll, and ran away. When the child reached the spot, she found the opening of a burrow, but the doll was not there. The child realized that the doll had fallen down the burrow, and she began to crawl inside. Neither the darkness around nor her many scratches made her despondent, and she crawled on until she reached a wide opening. She climbed through the opening, and there, before her eyes, was a magnificent palace surrounded by a lovely garden. And just near the opening of the burrow lay her doll. The child had not eaten anything all day, and she felt very hungry, so she entered the palace in search of food. She found there two large rooms; in the first one there was a table laden with ten dishes of food, and in the second one ten beds made up for the night. When the child approached the table, she heard voices from outside, so she hid herself under one of the beds. Suddenly into the room crawled ten huge serpents, terrible to behold.

The terrified child was on the point of screaming when the serpents shook themselves and shed their skins. They were no longer serpents but ten handsome young men, and they threw their skins out of the window. Then they knelt down and prayed, a prayer no less strange than anything the child had already seen. And these were the words of the prayer: "We pray for a fair maiden to come hither, burn our skins, and rescue us."

After praying, the young men ate their fill and then went to bed. As the child hid under one of the beds, she saw the man sleeping above her take out a handkerchief from his pocket and kiss it. The child immediately recognized whose handkerchief it was. She was very tired and fell asleep. In the morning, when she awoke, the serpents had vanished. So the girl left the palace and set off for the town, looking carefully in all directions so as to remember the way. She decided to go straight to the merchant's daughter and tell her of the handkerchief and all that she had seen; so she did. Immediately both of them ran together to the underground palace and hid themselves under one of the beds.

Everything happened as on the previous evening. When the serpents changed into men, the merchant's daughter recognized her beloved husband immediately. She waited patiently till nightfall, and when the young men were asleep, she went outside and burned their skins.

Morning came and the youths arose and saw what had happened. How they danced for joy! The merchant's daughter embraced her husband, and this is the story he told her: "We were ten princes. Our mother died, and our father remarried and had another son. Our stepmother bewitched all of us to ensure that her own son would succeed to the throne. Now that our skins have been burned, the witch has also been burned, and her spell is broken."

The same night the merchant dreamed of the same old man who had given him the diamond in a dream. The old man now freed him from his vow.

A wonderful wedding was arranged that same day, and people came from near and from far. When the old king died, the young couple succeeded to the throne, and they were beloved by all because they lived modestly, gave charity freely, and dealt out justice all the days of their life.

COMMENT: Recorded in Israel by Abraham Shani from a Jewish washerwoman born in Bukhara, "The Ten Serpents" is one of the many Cupid and Psyche tales distributed throughout Asia, including India, Turkey, Palestinian Arab groups, Iraq, and the Caucasus. The feature that makes this variant unusual is a child's search for her doll, which leads the heroine on a brave underground mission to free her husband and his nine brothers from their enchantment.

Eglė, Queen of Serpents

Lithuanian

*O*nce upon a time, there was an old man and an old woman. Together they had 12 sons and 3 daughters, the youngest of whom was called Eglė [Fir Tree]. One summer night the three sisters went bathing in the lake. After splashing around and washing themselves, they went back to the bank to get dressed. The youngest one noticed that a snake had wound himself in the sleeve of her shirt. The oldest girl grabbed a stick, ready to shoo the snake away. At that moment the snake, turning to the youngest girl, spoke in a human voice, "Give me, Eglutė [little Eglė], your word that you will marry me, then I will willingly slither out," he said.

Eglė started to cry. How could she marry a snake? Then she said, firmly, "Give back my shirt and go back where you came from."

"Give me your word that you will marry me," he said, "then I will willingly slither out."

What could she do? The word had to be given. Eglė promised to marry Žaltys [Serpent]. Three days later her parents noticed that a teeming group of snakes had slithered into their yard. Everyone was afraid, and no one knew what to do. Meanwhile, the snakes slithered about the yard, hissing, winding, and writhing. Two matchmaker snakes slunk into the house to speak to Eglė and her parents. Her parents were wary at first. They didn't want to comply, but what could they do? Unwillingly, they gave up their daughter. The snakes, having obtained the bride, slithered out of the yard. Her family cried and grieved.

Then Eglė and all the snakes headed toward the sea. There, she met a handsome prince, waiting for her. He told her he was the same serpent she had found in her shirt-sleeve. Soon they carried themselves to a nearby island and from there descended underwater, under the sea, to the magnificently adorned castle of the serpent prince, Žaltys. Here they held the wedding—they drank, danced, and reveled for three weeks.

Žaltys' castle was filled with everything one could ever ask for. No one had to work—there was complete freedom; you could only lounge around and be happy. So Eglė relaxed, cheered up, and after a while completely forgot about her home. Nine years trickled by. Eglė had three sons, Oak, Ash, and Birch—and one daughter, Aspen, who was the youngest. One day, the oldest son asked Eglė, "Mommy, where are your parents? Let's go visit them."

So she remembered once again her parents, brothers, sisters, and her home. She became concerned with how they were doing; whether they were healthy, alive, or perhaps already dead. Wanting to go home, she complained to her husband. She hadn't been home for so long, hadn't seen her loved ones, and missed them very much. Žaltys was skeptical.

"Fine," he said, "I will let you visit, but first you must spin this silk tow [unweavable coarse, broken fibers]," and he showed her the spinning wheel.

Žaltys' wife spun day and night. She spun and spun, but the pile of silk tow never shrank. She saw that she had been tricked; the tow had been bewitched. Spin as she might, she could never finish spinning. So Eglė visited an old woman who lived nearby—she was a sorceress. Having arrived, Eglė said, "Grandmother, for goodness sake, teach me how to spin that tow." The old one immediately explained what needed to be done and how.

"When you are preparing your cooking fire, throw it in. Otherwise, you'll never finish spinning."

Eglė went home and threw the tow in the stove, which had been prepared for bread-baking. Tow burned away, and Eglė saw a toad, as big as a clotheswashing paddle, squirming around in the fire. The bewitched toad had been spitting silk out of himself. Having dispatched both the toad and the spinning, Eglė again begged her husband to let her go home for at least a few days. Now, her husband pulled a pair of iron shoes from under a bench and said, "When you wear these out you can go home."

Wearing the shoes, she walked, stomped, and dragged them against rocks and bricks everywhere she could, but the shoes were thick and hard and would not wear out. It was obvious that they would last forever no matter what she did. She went again to the sorceress asking for help. The old woman advised her to take the shoes to a blacksmith and ask him to burn them with a hot poker. She did just that. The shoes burned sufficiently, and in three days Eglė was able to tear them apart. Having done so, she asked her husband to let her visit her parents.

"Fine," said Žaltys, "but before going you must bake a cake, for what will you bring to your nieces and nephews for treats?" And he commanded her to remove all her cooking utensils so it would be more difficult to bake. Eglė couldn't think of how to carry water without a bucket, nor mix dough for cake without any crockery, so she visited the sorceress once again. The sorceress said, "Take the leftover dough which you use to start each new loaf and spread it inside a sieve, and with that sieve you will be able to carry water and mix a new batch of dough."

So Žaltys' wife did this. She spread a sieve with dough to carry water and was able to bake a cake. After baking, she bid her husband and neighbors farewell and with her children left for home. Her husband accompanied them to the seashore and said that she could visit no longer than three times three days and then had to return immediately with her children. "On the way back, walk alone with your children, and upon reaching the seashore call me in this way:

Žaltys, my darling Žaltys!
If you are alive, foam milk before me,
And if you are dead, foam blood before me!

"And if you see white foam," he said, "then know that I am still alive, and if red foam—I have met my end. And you, children, don't you dare tell how to summon me." Having said this, he said goodbye to the children and expressed his hopes for their safe return.

At home, indescribable joy greeted Eglė. All of her neighbors and family gathered to meet her. Each person asked what it was like to live with the snakes. She told story after story. Each one plied her with refreshments and spoke to her with words of love. She hardly noticed how quickly those nine days leapt by. Her brothers, sisters, and parents tried to figure out what could be done to keep her from going back. Most important, they agreed that they needed to find out the name of Eglė's husband and how she would call for him at the seashore.

"We'll find all this out, go to the shore, call him, and kill him," they said. Having agreed on this, they first led Eglė's oldest son into the forest and questioned him, but he insisted that he knew nothing.

"I don't know," he said, and that was all.

They whipped him with a switch, but they couldn't get anything out of him. They warned him not to tell his mother anything when they let him go. On the second day they questioned Ash, then Birch, but couldn't get anything out of them, either. Finally, they beguiled Eglė's youngest daughter, Aspen. At first, she said she didn't know anything, but upon seeing the switch she told everything.

Soon after, all twelve brothers, with their scythes, went to the seashore. They stood on the beach and called:

Žaltys, my darling Žaltys!
If you are alive, foam milk before me,
And if you are dead, foam blood before me!

As soon as Žaltys swam ashore all the men attacked him and chopped him up. Later, at home, they did not tell Eglė what they had done.

So the nine days went by. Eglė bid everyone farewell, went to the seashore and called her husband:

Žaltys, my darling Žaltys!
If you are alive, foam milk before me,
And if you are dead, foam blood before me!

Eglė, Queen of Serpents

127

Gleaming ominously, the sea stirred, churning from its depths, and Eglė saw bloody foam swelling ashore, caressing the land, and she heard her husband's voice: "Your twelve brothers chopped me up with their scythes. Our most-loved daughter, Aspen, told them my secret!"

Eglė began to cry, and turning to her children, said:

> *Turn into an aspen tree*
> *So that you will tremble day and night*
> *So that rain will wash out your mouth*
> *And wind will comb your hair!*
> *Stand, my sons, as strong trees*
> *I, your mother, will remain a fir tree.*

What she said happened. The oak, ash, and birch are our strongest trees, and still today the aspen, touched by the slightest breeze, starts suddenly to tremble.

COMMENT: Lithuania leads Europe in hosting variants of "Beauty and the Beast," with thirty listed in Stith Thompson's *Types of the Folktale* (fifteen for Cupid and Psyche). "Eglė, Queen of Serpents," like the Japanese "Monkey Son-in-law," is included here for contrast to happy transformations, but this is not a trickster tale; it's a pourquoi tale with tragic proportions. Although the Beauty here does not betray her animal-husband, their daughter, who serves as the Beauty's double (two people often represent the same aspect in folklore), does.

Homely Women and Homemade Men

Sir Gawain and the Loathly Lady

English

*N*ow if you listen awhile I will tell you a tale of Arthur the King and how an adventure once befell him.

Of all kings and all knights, King Arthur bore away the honor wherever he went. In all his country there was nothing but chivalry, and knights were loved by the people.

One day in spring King Arthur was hunting in Ingleswood with all his lords beside him. Suddenly a deer ran by in the distance and the king took up chase, calling back to his knights, "Hold you still every man, I will chase this one myself!"

He took his arrows and bow and stooped low like a woodsman to stalk the deer. But every time he came near the animal, it leapt away into the forest. So King Arthur went a while after the deer, and no knight went with him, until at last he let fly an arrow and killed the deer. He had raised a bugle to his lips to summon the knights when he heard a voice behind him.

"Well met, King Arthur!"

Though he had not heard anyone approach, the king turned to see a strange knight, fully armed, standing only a few yards away.

"You have done me wrong many a year and given away my northern lands," said the strange knight. "I have your life in my hands—what will you do now, King Alone?"

"Sir Knight, what is your name?" asked the king.

"My name is Gromer Somer Joure."

"Sir Gromer, think carefully," said the king. "To slay me here, unarmed as I am, will get you no honor. All knights will refuse you wherever you go. Calm yourself—come to Carlyle and I shall mend all that is amiss."

"Nay," said Sir Gromer, "by heaven, King! You shall not escape when I have you at advantage. If I let you go with only a warning, later you'll defy me, of that I'm sure."

"Spare my life Sir Gromer, and I shall grant you whatever is in my power to give. It is shameful to slay me here, with nothing but my hunting gear, and you armed for battle."

"All your talking will not help you, King, for I want neither land nor gold, truly." Sir Gromer smiled. "Still . . . if you will promise to meet me here, in the same fashion, on a day I will choose . . ."

"Yes," said the king quickly. "Here is my promise."

"Listen and hear me out. First you will swear upon my sword to meet me here without fail, on this day one year from now. Of all your knights none shall come with you. You must tell me at your coming what thing women most desire—and if you do not bring the answer to my riddle, you will lose your head. What say you, King?"

"I agree, though it is a hateful bargain," said the king. "Now let me go. I promise you as I am the true king, to come again at this day one year from now and bring you your answer."

The knight laughed, "Now go your way, King Arthur. You do not yet know your sorrow. Yet stay a moment—do not think of playing false—for by Mary I think you would betray me."

"Nay," said King Arthur. "You will never find me an untrue knight. Farewell, Sir Knight, and evil met. I will come in a year's time, though I may not escape." The king began to blow his bugle for his knights to find him. Sir Gromer turned his horse and was gone as quickly as he had come, so that the lords found their king alone with the slain deer.

"We will return to Carlyle," said the king. "I do not like this hunting."

The lords knew by his countenance that the king had met with some disturbance, but no one knew of his encounter. They wondered at the king's heavy step and sad look, until at last Sir Gawain said to the king, "Sire, I marvel at you. What thing do you sorrow for?"

"I'll tell you, gentle Gawain," said Arthur. "In the forest as I pursued the deer, I met with a knight in full armor, and he charged me I should not escape him. I must keep my word to him or else I am foresworn."

"Fear not my lord. I am not a man that would dishonor you."

"He threatened me, and would have slain me with great heat, but I spoke with him since I had no weapons."

"What happened then?" said Gawain.

"He made me swear to meet him there in one year's time, alone and unarmed. On that day I must tell him what women desire most, or I shall lose my life. If I fail in my answer, I know that I will be slain without mercy."

"Sire, make good cheer," said Gawain. "Make your horse ready to ride into strange country, and everywhere you meet either man or woman, ask of them the answer to the riddle. I will ride another way, and every man and woman's answer I will write in a book."

"That is well advised, Gawain," said the king. They made preparations to leave immediately, and when both were ready, Gawain rode one way and the king another—each one asked every man and woman they found what women most desire.

Some said they loved beautiful clothes; some said they loved to be praised; some said they loved a handsome man; some said one, some said another. Gawain had so many answers that he made a great book to hold them, and after many months of traveling he came back to court again. The king was there already with his book, and each looked over the other's work. But no answer seemed right.

"By God," said the king, "I am afraid. I will seek a little more in Ingleswood Forest. I have but one month to my set day, and I may find some good tidings."

"Do as you think best," said Gawain, "but whatever you do, remember that it is good to have spring again."

King Arthur rode forth on that day, into Ingleswood, and there he met with a lady. King Arthur marveled at her, for she was the ugliest creature that he had ever seen. Her face seemed almost like that of an animal, with a pushed-in nose and a few yellowing tusks for teeth. Her figure was twisted and deformed, with a hunched back and shoulders a yard broad. No tongue could tell the foulness of that lady. But she rode gaily on a palfrey set with gold and precious stones, and when she spoke her voice was sweet and soft.

"I am glad that I have met with you, King Arthur," she said. "Speak with me, for your life is in my hand. I know of your situation, and I warn you that you will not find your answer if I do not tell you."

"What do you want with me, lady?" said the king, taken aback by the lady's boldness.

"Sir, I would like to speak with you. You will die if I do not save you, I know it very well."

"What do you mean my lady, tell me," stammered the king. "What is your desire, why is my life in your hand? Tell me, and I shall give you all you ask."

"You must grant me a knight to wed," said the lady slowly. "His name is Sir Gawain. I will make this bargain: if your life is saved another way, you need not grant my desire. If my answer saves your life, grant me Sir Gawain as my husband. Choose now, for you must soon meet your enemy."

"By Mary," said the king, "I cannot grant you Sir Gawain. That lies with him alone—he is not mine to give. I can only take the choice to Sir Gawain."

"Well," she said. "Then go home again and speak to Sir Gawain. For though I am foul, yet am I merry, and through me he may save your life or ensure your death."

"Alas!" cried the king. "That I should cause Gawain to wed you, for he will not say no. I know not what I should do."

"Sir King, you will get no more from me. When you come again with your answer I will meet you here."

"What is your name, I pray you tell me?"

"Sir King, I am the Dame Ragnell, that never yet betrayed a man."

"Then farewell, Dame Ragnell," said the king.

Thus they departed, and the king returned to Carlyle again with a heavy heart.

The first man he met was Sir Gawain. "Sire, how did you fare?" asked the knight.

"Never so ill," said the king. "I fear I will die at Sir Gromer's hand."

"Nay," said Gawain. "I would rather die myself I love you so."

"Gawain, I met today with the foulest lady that I ever saw. She said she would save my life, but first she would have you for her husband."

"Is this all?" asked Gawain. "Then I shall wed her and wed her again! Though she were a fiend, though she were as foul as Beelzebub, her I shall marry. For you are my king and I am your friend—it is my part to save your life, or else I am a false knight and a great coward. If she were the most loathsome woman that ever a man might see, for your love I would spare nothing."

"Thank you Gawain," said King Arthur then. "Of all knights that I have found, you are the finest. You have saved my life, and my love will not stray from you, as I am king in this land."

The day soon came when the king was to meet the Dame Ragnell and bear his answer to Sir Gromer. Gawain rode with him to the edge of Ingleswood Forest, but there the king said, "Sir Gawain, farewell. I must go west, and you must go no further."

"God speed you on your journey. I wish I rode your way." said Gawain.

The king had ridden but a mile or so more when he met the Dame Ragnell. "Ah, Sir King, you are welcome here bearing your answer."

"Now," said the king, "since it can be no other way, tell me your answer, save my life, and Gawain shall you wed; so he has promised. Tell me in all haste. Have done, I may not tarry."

"Sire," said the Dame Ragnell, "now you will know what women desire most, high and low. Some men say we desire to be fair, or to wed, or to remain fresh and young, or to have flattery from men. But there is one thing that is every woman's fantasy: we desire of men, above all other things, to have sovereignty, for then all is ours. Therefore go on your way, Sir King, and tell that knight what I have said to you. He will be angry and curse the woman who told you, for his labor is lost. Go forth—you will not be harmed."

The king rode forth in great haste until he came to the set place and met with Sir Gromer.

"Come, come, Sir King," said the knight sternly. "Now let me have your answer, for I am ready."

The king pulled out the two books for Sir Gromer to see. "Sir, I dare say the right one is there."

Sir Gromer looked over them, every one, and said at last, "Nay nay, Sir King, you are a dead man."

"Wait, Sir Gromer," said the king. "I have one more answer to give."

"Say it," said Sir Gromer, "or so God help me you shall bleed."

"Now," said the king, "here is my answer and that is all—above all things, women desire sovereignty, for that is their liking and their greatest desire; to rule over any man. This they told me."

Sir Gromer was silent a moment with rage, but then he cried out, "And she that told you, Sir Arthur, I pray to God I might see her burn in a fire, for that was my sister, Dame Ragnell. God give her shame—I have lost much labor. Go where you like, King Arthur, for you are spared. Alas that I ever saw this day, for I know that you will be my enemy and hunt me down."

"No," said King Arthur, "you will never find me an attacker. Farewell." King Arthur turned his horse into the forest again. Soon he met with the Dame Ragnell, in the same place as before. "Sir King," she said. "I am glad you have sped well. I told you how it would be, and now since I and none other have saved your life, Gawain must wed me."

"I will not fail in my promise," said the king. "If you will be ruled by my council, you shall have your will."

"No, Sir King, I will not be ruled," said the Lady. "I know what you are thinking. Ride before, and I will follow to your court. Think how I have saved your life and do not disagree with me, for if you do you will be shamed."

The king was ashamed to bring the loathly lady openly to the court, but forth she rode till they came to Carlyle. All the country wondered when she came, for they had never seen so foul a creature, but she would spare no one the sight of her. Into the hall she went, saying, "Arthur, King, fetch in Sir Gawain, before all the knights, so that you may troth us together. Set forth Gawain my love, for I will not wait."

Sir Gawain and the Loathly Lady

Sir Gawain stepped forward then, and said, "Sir, I am ready to fulfill the promise I made to you."

"God have mercy," said the Dame Ragnell when she saw Gawain. "For your sake I wish I were a fair woman, for you are of such good will." Then Sir Gawain wooed her as he was a true knight, and Dame Ragnell was happy.

"Alas!" said the Queen Guinevere, and all the ladies in her bower. "Alas!" said both king and knights, that the beautiful Gawain should wed such a foul and horrible woman.

She would be wedded in no other way than this—openly, with announcements in every town and village, and she had all the ladies of the land come to Carlyle for the feast. The queen begged Dame Ragnell to be married in the early morning, as privately as possible. "Nay," said the lady. "By heaven I will not no matter what you say. I will be wedded openly, as the king promised. I will not go to the church until high-mass time, and I will dine in the open hall, in the midst of all the court."

At the wedding feast there were lords and ladies from all estates, and Dame Ragnell was arrayed in the richest manner—richer even than Queen Guinevere. But all her rich clothes could not hide her foulness. When the feasting began, only Dame Ragnell ate heartily, while the knights and squires sat like stones. After the wedding feast, Sir Gawain and the Lady Ragnell retired to the wedding chamber that had been prepared for them.

"Ah, Gawain," said the lady. "Since we are wed, show me your courtesy and come to bed. If I were fair you would be joyous—yet for Arthur's sake kiss me at least."

Sir Gawain turned to the lady, but in her place was the loveliest woman that he had ever seen.

"By God, what are you?" cried Gawain.

"Sir, I am your wife, surely. Why are you so unkind?"

"Lady, I am sorry," said Gawain. "I beg your pardon, my fair madam. For now you are a beautiful lady, and today you were the foulest woman that ever I saw. It is well, my lady, to have you thus." And he took her in his arms and kissed her with great joy.

"Sir," she said, "you have half-broken the spell on me. Thus shall you have me, but my beauty will not hold. You may have me fair by night and foul by day, or else have me fair by day, and by night ugly once again. You must choose."

"Alas!" said Gawain, "The choice is too hard—to have you fair on nights and no more, that would grieve my heart and shame me. Yet if I desire to have you fair by day and foul by night I could not rest. I know not in the world what I should say, but do as you wish. The choice is in your hands."

"Thank you, courteous Gawain," said the lady. "Of all earthly knights you are blessed, for now I am truly loved. You shall have me fair both day and night, and ever while I live as fair. For I was shaped by witchcraft by my stepmother, God have mercy on her. By enchantment I was to be the foulest creature, till the best knight of England had wedded me and had given me the sovereignty of all his body and goods. Kiss me, Sir Gawain—be glad and make good cheer, for we are well." The two rejoiced together and thanked God for their fortune.

King Arthur came himself to call them to breakfast the next day, wondering why Gawain stayed so late with his loathly bride. Sir Gawain rose, taking the hand of his lady, and opened the door to greet the king.

The Dame Ragnell stood by the fire, with pale lovely skin and red hair spilling down to her knees. "Lo," said Gawain to the king, "this is my wife the Dame Ragnell, who once saved your life." And Gawain told the king the story of the lady's enchantment.

"My love shall she have, for she has been so kind," said the king. And the queen said, "You have my love forever, Lady, for you have saved my Lord Arthur." And from then on, at every great feast, that lady was the fairest, and all his life Gawain loved the Lady Ragnell.

Thus ends the adventure of King Arthur and of the wedding of Sir Gawain.

COMMENT: This Arthurian romance, adapted from a medieval poem titled "The Wedding of Sir Gawain and Dame Ragnell," is striking in its emphasis on the importance of a woman's power to control her own choices. The horrific but heroic female saves a king's life, outwits a sorcerer, wins a husband worthy of her, and reforms him even as he transforms her. The nineteenth-century English folklorist Joseph Jacobs suggests that Gawain may be Owein, the hero of "The Laidley Worm," as well as Owyne, the hero of "Kemp Owyne." Both the ballads and the legend are included here to show the variety in this Celtic transformation story, identified as tale type 402A.

The Laidley Worm of Spindleston Heughs

Scottish

*T*he king is gone from Bambrough castle,
Long may the princess mourn;
Long may she stand on the castle wall,
Looking for his return.

She has knotted the keys upon a string,
And with her she has them taken,
She has cast them over her left shoulder,
And to the gate has hastened.

She tripped out, she tripped in,
She tripped into the yard;
But it was more for the king's sake,
Than for the queen's regard.

It fell out on a day the king
Brought the queen with him home,
And all the lords in our country
To welcome them did come.

"O welcome, father," the lady cries,
"Unto your halls and bowers;
And so are you, my stepmother,
For all that is here is yours."

A lord said, wondering while she spoke,
This princess of the North
Surpasses all of female kind
In beauty and in worth.

The envious queen replied: "At least,
You might have excepted me;
In a few hours I will her bring
Down to a low degree.

"I will her liken to a laidley worm,
That warps about the stone,
And not till Childy Wynd comes back
Shall she again be won."

The princess stood at the bower door,
Laughing, who could her blame?
But 'ere the next day's sun went down,
A long worm she became.

For seven miles east, and seven miles west,
And seven miles north and south,
No blade of grass or corn could grow,
So venomous was her mouth.

The milk of seven stately cows—
It was costly her to keep—
Was brought her daily, which she drank
Before she went to sleep.

At this day may be seen the cave
Which held her folded up,
And the stone trough, the very same
Out of which she did sup.

Word went east, and word went west,
And word is gone over the sea,
That a laidley worm in Spindleston
Heughs
Would ruin the north country.

Word went east, and word went west,
And over the sea did go;
The Child of Wynd got wit of it,
Which filled his heart with woe.

He called straight his merry men all,
They thirty were and three:
"I wish I were at Spindleston,
This desperate worm to see.

"We have no time now here to waste,
Hence quickly let us sail;
My only sister Margaret,
Something, I fear, doth ail."

They built a ship without delay,
With masts of the rowan tree,
With fluttering sails of silk so fine,
And set her on the sea.

They went aboard; the wind with speed
Blew them along the deep;
At length they spied a huge square tower,
On a rock high and steep.

The sea was smooth, the weather clear;
When they approached nigher,
King Ida's castle they well knew,
And the banks of Bambroughshire.

The queen looked out at her bower-window,
To see what she could see;
There she espied a gallant ship,
Sailing upon the sea.

When she beheld the silken sails,
Full glancing in the sun,
To sink the ship she sent away
Her witch-wives every one.

Their spells were vain; the hags returned
To the queen in sorrowful mood,
Crying that witches have no power
Where there is rowan-tree wood.

Her last effort, she sent a boat,
Which in the haven lay,
With armed men to board the ship,
But they were driven away.

The worm leapt up, the worm leapt
down,
She plaited round the stone;
And aye as the ship came to the land
She banged it off again.

The Child then ran out of her reach
The ship on Budle sand,
And jumping into the shallow sea,
Securely got to land.

And now he drew his berry-brown sword,
And laid it on her head,
And swore, if she did harm to him,
That he would strike her dead

"O quit thy sword, and bend thy bow,
And give me kisses three;
For though I am a poisonous worm,
No hurt I will do to thee.

"O quit thy sword, and bend thy bow,
And give me kisses three;
If I am not won ere the sun go down,
Won I shall never be."

He quitted his sword, he bent his bow,
He gave her kisses three;
She crept into a hole a worm,
But stepped out a lady.

No clothing had this lady fine,
To keep her from the cold;
He took his mantle from him about,
And round her did it fold.

He has taken his mantle from him about,
And it he wrapped her in,
And they are up to Bambrough castle,
As fast as they can win.

His absence and her serpent shape
The king had long deplored;
He now rejoiced to see them both
Again to him restored.

The queen they wanted, whom they found
All pale, and sore afraid,
Because she knew her power must yield
To Childy Wynd's, who said:

"Woe be to thee, thou wicked witch,
An ill death mayest thou die;
As thou my sister hast likened,
So likened shalt thou be.

"I will turn you into a toad,
That on the ground doth wend,
And won, won shalt thou never be,
Till this world hath an end."

Now on the sand near Ida's tower,
She crawls a loathsome toad,
And venom spits on every maid
She meets upon her road.

The virgins all of Bambrough town
Will swear that they have seen
This spiteful toad of monstrous size,
While walking they have been.

All folks believe within the shire
This story to be true,
And they all run to Spindleston,
The cave and trough to view.

This fact now Duncan Frasier,
Of Cheviot, sings in rhyme,
Lest Bambroughshire men should forget
Some part of it in time.

COMMENTS: Included in volume I of *English and Scottish Popular Ballads*, edited in 1882 by Francis James Child, this is an eighteenth-century ballad based on the more ancient "Kempion" or "Kemp Owyne," which is also included here. Kemp, or Champion, Owain was a Welsh hero of the sixth century whose name was corrupted to Childey Wynd or Child of Wynde. The Laidley Worm is a loathsome dragon. The transformation of young women who have been enchanted in the form of animals—often snakes—is common in almost as broad a range of folklore as is the transformation of enchanted young men. Here, the loving loyalty that saves the beast depends on a bond between sister and brother instead of wife and husband. A related Icelandic saga, however, has the enchanted woman transformed by a hero who later marries her.

Kemp Owyne

Scottish

*H*er mother died when she was young,
Which gave her cause to make great moan;
Her father married the worst woman
That ever lived in Christendom.

She served her with foot and hand,
In every thing that she could do,
Till once, in an unlucky time,
She threw her in over Craigy's sea.

Says, "Lie you there, dove Isabel,
And all my sorrows lie with thee;
Till Kemp Owyne come over the sea,

And borrow you with kisses three,
Let all the world do what they will,
Oh borrowed shall you never be!"

Her breath grew strange, her hair grew long,
And twisted thrice about the tree,
And all the people, far and near,
Thought that a savage beast was she.

These news did come to Kemp Owyne,
Where he lived, far beyond the sea;
He hastened him to Craigy's sea,
And on the savage beast looked he.

Her breath was strange, her hair was long,
And twisted was about the tree,
And with a swing she came about:
"Come to Craigy's sea, and kiss with me.

"Here is a royal belt," she cried,
"That I have found in the green sea;
And while your body it is on,
Drawn shall your blood never be;
But if you touch me, tail or fin,
I vow my belt your death shall be."

He stepped in, gave her a kiss,
The royal belt he brought him with;
Her breath was strange, her hair was long,
And twisted twice about the tree,
And with a swing she came about:
"Come to Craigy's sea, and kiss with me.

"Here is a royal ring," she said,
"That I have found in the green sea;
And while your finger it is on,
Drawn shall your blood never be;
But if you touch me, tail or fin,
I swear my ring your death shall be."

He stepped in, gave her a kiss,
The royal ring he brought him with;
Her breath was strange, her hair was
long,
And twisted once about the tree,
And with a swing she came about:
"Come to Craigy's sea, and kiss with me.

"Here is a royal brand," she said,
"That I have found in the green sea;
And while your body it is on,
Drawn shall your blood never be;
But if you touch me, tail or fin,
I swear my brand your death shall be."

He stepped in, gave her a kiss,
The royal brand he brought him with;
Her breath was sweet, her hair grew
short,
And twisted none about the tree,
And smilingly she came about,
As fair a woman as fair could be.

Pinto Smalto

Italian

*T*here was once a merchant with an only daughter, for whom he greatly desired to find a husband, but she resented the approach of any man. She wished only to get what she wanted, which made her father the most miserable and afflicted man in the world.

One day, when he was going to market, he asked Betta (such was his daughter's name) what she would like him to bring her back on his return, and she answered, "Papa, if you love me, bring me half a quintal of

Palermo sugar and half of ambrosian almonds, five or six flagons of scented water, a little musk and amber, about two score pearls, two sapphires, a handful of garnets and rubies with a little spun gold, and above all a modeling bowl and a silver scalpel."

Her father was amazed at this extravagant request, but, not wishing to disoblige her, he went to the fair and on his return brought her just what she had asked for. As soon as she had received them, she shut herself into a room and began to make a great quantity of paste with the sugar and almonds, mixed with the rose-water and perfumes, and with this she started to model a handsome youth, giving him locks of spun gold, eyes of sapphire, teeth of pearls, lips of rubies, and all this with such grace and beauty that only speech was lacking.

Betta had heard that a statue had once come to life through the prayers of a certain king of Cyprus, so, when she had finished her work, she prayed so earnestly to the Goddess of Love that her statue began to open its eyes and then to breathe, and following breath came out words, and at last, disengaging its limbs, it began to walk.

Betta was more overjoyed than if she had won a kingdom. She threw her arms round him and kissed him, then, taking him by the hand, she led him to her father and said, "My good papa, you have always said you wanted to see me married, so to please you I have chosen the husband of my heart."

When her father saw this handsome young man, whom he had not previously seen enter, coming out of his daughter's room, he was filled with amazement. But when he perceived his marvelous beauty, which one would willingly pay a grain a head for admission to gaze at, he decided to consent to the marriage.

At the splendid feasts held to celebrate the wedding, there chanced to be a great queen incognita among the many others who came to take part. She was so struck with admiration at the beauty of Pinto Smalto (such was the name Betta had given him) that she was seized with an unfeigned love for him. Pinto Smalto, whose eyes had opened to the wickedness of the world but three hours before, knew no troubled waters, so when, as his bride directed him, he accompanied the departing guests to the foot of the stairs and was in this way escorting the strange lady, she took him by the hand and led him gently to her carriage, with its six horses, which was waiting in the courtyard, and drew him in. She ordered the coachman to drive off at a gallop in the direction of her lands, where the simple Pinto Smalto, not knowing what had befallen him, became her husband.

Betta waited some time for him. Then, seeing that he did not return, she sent down to the courtyard to find out if anyone was holding him in conversation. She sent, too, to the roof terrace in case he had gone there for a breath of air, and she herself went to the privy to see if he had gone to pay his first tribute to the necessities of life. But he was nowhere to be found, so she imagined that he had been stolen away from her because of his great beauty. She had the usual proclamations spread abroad, but since no one came forward to reveal his hiding place, she determined to go in search of him herself, disguised as a beggar.

She set out on her way, and after several months she came to the house of a good old woman who received her with great kindness. She was so sorry for Betta when she heard of her misfortunes and saw that she was pregnant that she taught her three phrases. The first was "Tricche-varlacche, for the house is raining"; the second "Anola tranola, pizza fontanola"; and the third "Tafaro tamburo, pizze 'ngongole e cemmino" [these are all nonsense chants in a children's game]. The old woman added that if she spoke these words in any moment of dire need, she would receive succor.

Although Betta was amazed at such a worthless gift, she said to herself, "He who spits in your face, does not wish you dead, and he who takes does not wither: every bit helps. Who knows what good fortune is hidden in these words!" So she thanked the old woman and went on her way.

After journeying a long time, she reached a fine city called Monterotondo and went straight to the royal palace, where she asked in Heaven's name for shelter, even in a stable, seeing that she was near the time of delivery.

The ladies of the court had pity on her and brought her into a little room under the stairs and while she was there, the unhappy girl saw Pinto Smalto pass by. Such was the weight of her joy that she nearly slipped down the tree of life.

Betta felt that this was indeed an hour of need, so, to test the first words taught her by the old woman, she said, "Tricche-varlacche, for the house is raining!" and at once there appeared before her a beautiful little golden cart glittering with gems, which ran by itself all round the room and was a marvel to behold.

The ladies who had seen this told the queen about it, and she, without a moment's delay, ran to Betta's room and, admiring her magnificent jewel, asked if she would sell it, because she would be paid any sum she demanded. But Betta answered that she held her own pleasures dearer than all the gold in the world and that if the queen wanted the little cart, she must allow her to sleep one night with her husband.

The queen was greatly surprised at the madness of this poor ragged girl, who for a whim gave away such riches. She made up her mind to win this tasty morsel and, by giving Pinto Smalto a dose of opium, content the girl and yet pay her ill. At nightfall, when the stars of heaven and the fireflies on earth come forth to show themselves, the queen gave Pinto Smalto a sleeping draught and sent him, obedient as he was, to sleep with Betta. But the young man, as soon as his head touched the pillow, was sleeping as fast as any dormouse.

The unhappy Betta, who had thought that night to repay herself for all her past woes, saw that she had not obtained a hearing. She began to lament unceasingly and reproached him with all that she had done for his good. But the sleeper did not once open his eyes, and the sorrowing girl did not once shut her mouth until the sun came up with his resin water to divide the shadows from the light. Then the queen entered and, taking Pinto Smalto by the hand, said to Betta, "Now you are satisfied!"

"May you too have such satisfaction all the days of your life!" said Betta to herself. "For I have passed such a bad night that I shan't forget it for many a day."

But she could not resist the urge of her longing, so she tried the second phrase, saying, "Anola tranola, pizza fontanola!" and there appeared to her a golden cage with a most lovely bird made from gold and precious stones that sang like any nightingale.

It all fell out as before. The ladies saw the wonderful object and told the queen, and she in her turn went to see it, made the same request, and received the same answer. She thought she had discovered the girl to be an easy gull, so she promised to let her sleep with her husband and so carried off the cage and bird. When night came, she gave the same soporific to Pinto Smalto and sent him to Betta in the same room, where she had had a magnificent bed set up. When poor Betta saw him sleeping as if he were dead, she again took up her lament, saying things that would have moved even the stones to pity, and so, groaning and weeping and tearing her hair, she passed another night of torment. At daybreak, the queen came in to reclaim her husband and left the miserable Betta cold and frozen, biting her hands in anger at the trick that had been played her a second time.

That same morning Pinto Smalto went to pick some figs in a garden outside the city gates, where he met a cobbler, who lived next to Betta's room and had heard every word she said through the walls. The cobbler repeated exactly the weeping and wailing and lamentation of the unhappy beggar. On hearing this, the king, who was already beginning to gather his wits, cast about in his mind to guess how this had chanced, so he decided that if he were sent another time to sleep with the poor girl, he would not swallow the potion that the queen had set before him.

Betta made her third trial and said, "Tafaro tamburo, pizze 'ngongole e cemmino!" and there appeared a quantity of silks and cloth of gold and embroidered linen with a golden cradle, so that even the queen herself would not have been able to show such finery. The ladies saw them and told their mistress, and she tried to bargain for them in the same way. At Betta's third request, she said to herself, "What do I lose by contenting this silly girl if I gain all these fine things?" So she took the riches that Betta offered her and, when night came, she gave Pinto Smalto the sleeping draught. But he kept it in his mouth and, pretending to go and empty his bowels, he spat it out. When he was in bed, Betta, who was at his side, began again her lament, saying how she had with her own hands modeled him from sugar and almonds, how she had given him golden hair and eyes and mouth of precious stones, how he was in her debt for the life that the gods had given him because of her prayers, how he had been stolen from her so that she had gone, heavy with child, in search of him through the world, suffering such hardships as she prayed Heaven to keep all Christian souls from, and, moreover, how she had already slept two nights with him and twice given away treasures in payment, and not one single word had he given her. This, then, would be the last night of her hopes and the last hour of her life.

Pinto Smalto was awake and heard her words. He recalled as if in a dream all that had happened and, embracing Betta, tried to console her as best he could. Then since Night, in her black mask, was directing the dance of the Stars, he crept out of bed and went very quietly to the queen's room, where he found her sunk in sleep. He took all the things she had torn from Betta and all the finery and jewels that were in the chest to repay them their past troubles and returned to his wife, and they both went away at once and traveled on until they passed the frontiers of that kingdom. They rested in a handsome lodging until Betta had given birth to her son, and as soon as she could leave her bed, they set off toward her father's house. They found him alive and in good health, and he was so overjoyed to see his daughter again that he lost years of his life and became like a boy of fifteen. The queen, when she found that her husband and the beggar and her jewels had all disappeared, tore her hair in rage and despair. But there were some who did not forbear to tell her that he who deceives must not complain of deceit.

COMMENT: A story from the *Pentamerone* (1634) by Giambattista Basile, this Italian variant of the wife's quest for her husband *begins* with a transformation, or rather a creation: the woman makes her man out of precious materials instead of accepting an animal foisted on her by a father who has gotten himself into trouble. However, the best-laid plans go wrong; the bride must win back her humanized robot, which she has made so cleverly to her own liking that someone else (reminiscent of the Troll princess and other assorted rivals for the animal groom's affection) likes him as well and steals him away. I have changed a few obscure phrases in the beginning, but otherwise the tale is complete.

The Dough Prince

West Virginian

*O*nce there was a princess who couldn't find a prince she could love, so she decided to make one. She mixed a dough and shaped it like a man: straight, tall, and very handsome. When the princess kissed him, he came to life. She taught him to talk and walk and he grew to be a fine young prince. They got married and she loved him more and more each day.

Because the bandits were causing a great deal of trouble in the country, the prince resolved to campaign against them and, in his pursuit, followed them out of the country. This made the princess very sad because she didn't want him to leave.

The prince, after many months of traveling, fell in with these thieves at a palace where they were hiding out, in some far-off land. The queen of the palace fell in love with him and forced him to marry her.

In order to keep the prince from escaping she kept him drugged by giving him wine just before bedtime.

In the meantime, the princess-wife, who had been left behind, decided to go out and hunt for her prince. After traveling for several months, she stopped to rest, and while she was resting, a little old man approached her. He told her where she could find her prince and gave her three valuable stones. The little man told her to show the smallest stone first.

The princess went to the palace as the little man had directed, sat under a tree in the courtyard, and got out the smallest stone to examine. It glittered in the sunlight and caught the eye of the queen, who told one of her servants to bring the girl to her. When the princess was asked what she wanted for the stone, she asked to be allowed to sleep with the queen's husband one night. At first the queen got angry and slapped her face, but remembering that he would be drugged, she consented.

That night the princess did everything in her power to awaken him but she did not succeed. One of the servants overheard her and told her she would help her if she could.

The next day the princess again sat in the courtyard and got out the second stone. This one was brighter than the first and it also caught the queen's eye. The princess again asked to sleep one night with her husband and the stone would be hers. The queen consented, but the same thing happened as before: the prince did not wake up.

The next day the princess brought out her last stone and again the queen wanted it. The girl asked for the same favor, which was granted. This time the servant, who had promised to help, switched bottles and gave him plain wine instead of the drugged wine. That night the princess woke him up and he realized she was his princess. The servant helped them to escape and had horses ready for them.

The prince later told all he knew about the bandits and got the people to rebel against them. With the bandits out of the way, they lived peaceably thereafter.

The Dough Prince

COMMENT: Here's a homespun Appalachian relative of Basile's heroine in "Pinto Smalto." This princess doesn't fool around with precious materials to make her man, but shapes him out of plain old dough. He seems to be just as satisfactory, however, if a trifle passive. Perhaps that's his main attraction for the active princess, who first kisses him to life, then saves him from a bandit queen.

Old Man Coyote, the Young Man and Two Otter Sisters

Native American

*O*nce upon a time there lived a young man who had riches as well as being handsome.

Old Man Coyote said to him one day, "You had better get married, and I will find you a suitable wife." One winter when the ice was all smooth and nice, the people of the earth were sitting on buffalo skulls (for sledges), while the young men pulled them over the ice.

The rich and handsome young man came to this place and saw two beautiful women he had never seen before. He approached them and subsequently pulled them over the ice on buffalo skulls until late, and after all the other people had gone home. These two beautiful women proved to be long otters with fine fur, who had been transformed into young and beautiful women (sisters) to ensnare a husband. As they were nearing an air hole, one of them threw her robe over the head of the young man, while the other sister pushed, so that all three of them went into the air hole. When he came to, he was sitting in a tipi under the water, where these women lived with their people.

While he was lying in the tipi with the two sisters that he had married, he could see people coming for water and could hear the camp criers announcing that they would have a buffalo hunt. One of his wives said, "You had better go and get some meat for us and our father." He went, leading a string of horses by a rope, and after a successful hunt, he loaded the horses with the choicest parts of the buffalo and took them to his wives after dark. He saw them sitting on the bank waiting for him. He told them to unload the horses, which they did, and they dumped the meat through the air hole. One of the wives took the horses to where his other horses were, and they then went under the water to their tipi to see his father-in-law, a large otter, eat. He was eating marrow, bones and all.

The following day, the husband of the two sisters went to his former camp and people and told the chief to have it announced that he was married to two women otters under the water, that his father-in-law never got enough to eat, and that he would have to have the whole camp go buffalo hunting again, which they did, with instructions to leave nothing behind, but bring everything, entrails and all.

A big killing was made, and when they returned, the procession was a very large one. The horses were unloaded of the results of the hunt on the edge of the air hole, until it made a big pile. When they had put all the meat in the air hole, the young man came out and announced that his father-in-law and the friends of his father-in-law would come and have a feast and that when they did come, they would break up the ice, so that the people had better camp on the hills. When the otters came, they broke up the ice and the water rushed on the ice and high on the banks, but the people were safe. The otters had a big feast.

Afterward the camp moved away, leaving the man with his wives and his father-in-law. His father-in-law told him to plait his scalp lock and tie the ends with otter skins and when-ever hunting, to watch out for the enemy, for they were watching him, and that when they came up to him he was to touch his scalp lock to the ground and he would disappear under the ground. But one day he was ambushed by his enemies and shot all over with arrows. He started to run, not thinking of his medicine (the otter skin). When he fell, his scalp locks touched the ground and he immediately disappeared under the ground and his medicine carried him home to his wives and father-in-law, where he was shortly restored to health.

His father-in-law said to him, "You have lived with me long enough. You must want to see your people now, so take your wives and go home to your people." Upon his return to his people he was made a chief, a leader in war, and every time a warrior was shot he was taken to the water and with his medicine cured.

One day one of his wives went home and the otter gave birth to a boy child. She said to him, "Don't call him a bad name, for if you do I will leave you." One day when he was angry, he did so, and she was transformed into an otter and went home under the water with her child. Her husband followed her, but he could no longer stay under the water as he used to and reached the bank almost drowned. He met Old Man Coyote, who said to him, "Put a lot of rocks in a bag and tie it around your neck." So he did this and went down under the water and barely came out alive. He then went to the river bank near the home of his wives and cried, and his father-in-law said to his daughters, "Take him back to his own people." But the daughters would not at first consent. At last the daughter without the child took him back, and they lived with each other happily afterward.

COMMENT: Collected from the Crow Indians of Montana in 1902, this story was related (through an interpreter) by Bull-That-Goes-Hunting, the second oldest man of his tribe. Although the pattern is obviously different from European, Asian, and African stories about animal husbands and wives, the themes are remarkably similar: a young person weds a creature (actually two) who is made human by the marriage. In this case, the beast is female, and the warrior must go to her underwater tipi, just as Beauty goes to the Beast's palace. There the young man is torn between the people in his former camp and the otters into whose clan he has married, just as Psyche and her many counterparts suffer split loyalties between a childhood family and a new marriage. The resolution is a happy compromise: he gains a human wife after learning to accept and respect the power of her animal kin. In two other Native American tales that have been adapted into popular picture books, *The Girl Who Loved Wild Horses* and *The Buffalo Wife* by Paul Goble, the human reconciles with his or her true love by becoming an animal. Coyote, by the way, is no more help to the young man in this story than the Greek gods were to Psyche or the French fairies to Beauty.

Essays, Activities, and Resources

In the Dark with Disney

Our lives are full of dark and scary journeys. The first is birth, when we're pressed from the cozy dark by forces beyond our control into a sudden realm of cold air, bright light, loud noise, and gnawing hunger. The only reassurance is love in the form of warm arms, low voices, and sweet milk. If that love is steady and consistent, it transforms us from helpless children into adults who have the power to love and nurture our own families. The love we receive as children helps us on many dark journeys, whether they're as brief as running down a haunted hallway to the bathroom at night or as endless as walking across a playground surrounded by taunting classmates.

The darkest journeys of all are within ourselves. Growing involves pain and fear on the way to happiness, and happiness is not usually what we expect it to be. Sometimes we don't even recognize it. What happens on a journey can change our destination. We arrive at a strange place that may seem frightening or magic or both. Loving someone can be a strange journey, with hardships along the way. Yet the deep acceptance in a loving relationship seems to transform us and light up the world.

All of the stories in this book except one, "The Monkey Son-in-law" (which I included for contrast), are about journeys in which the heroine or hero is transformed not through winning battles but through love for another being. Fighting, overcoming, and killing monsters is an essential

element of many tales, from "Jack the Giant Killer" to "St. George and the Dragon"; but in the stories here, the point is to understand the monster and see what he or she is really like underneath a frightening appearance. Beauty and the Beast tales suggest, among other things, that love is as powerful as force in coming to terms with what we fear.

Folktales mean many different things at different times to different audiences, who shape and reshape a story depending on what they remember or consider important. Jan-Öjvind Swahn researched his book *The Tale of Cupid and Psyche* (Gleerup, 1955) for twenty years to identify and analyze cultural variations of that particular tale type. The variants he looked at, however, were passed slowly among small groups that were often socially related. What happens when one form of a tale suddenly takes over an audience of millions the way Disney's animated film of Beauty and the Beast has? No one really knows because mass media are new, whereas the stories in this collection have already lasted for centuries.

While I was attending an opera of Beauty and the Beast called "Desert of Roses," composed by Robert Moran and performed for the first time by the Houston Opera Company in 1991, I overheard a man behind me whisper to his companion, "Where's Gaston?" I wanted to turn around and tell him, "Gaston is not part of the fairy tale. The Disney film has added Gaston to kill the Beast. And has subtracted Beauty's sisters. And, in the fairy tale, the Beast never fights with wolves or gets stabbed in the back, and the magic objects in the castle never fight with the townspeople, and no evil insane-asylum director ever threatens to take Beauty's father away to an institution. And no teacup named Chip rescues Beauty. In the fairy tale, Beauty starts the action by asking for a rose. And the Beast almost dies because Beauty has gone away and left him, not because a rival stabs him in the back while Beauty watches helplessly from the sidelines."

But, of course, I did not say any of those things because people were singing on stage, and I didn't want to interrupt them. And anyway, what difference would it have made? Beauties and Beasts have survived worse. Well, it might make a difference to you sometime on a dark journey. Would you rather try to win a monster with love or overcome a monster with hate? Even the monsters inside of you have to be tamed slowly, with acceptance and love, as the Beast was. They can't just be killed off in one climactic fight like Gaston, hurled to his death.

We are all beautiful and we are all beastly. That is an important focus of a Beauty and Beast story, and teacups dis-tract from that focus considerably. None of us is made of china. As an image, teacups just aren't in the same league with a love-or-death struggle. Dancing forks and spoons make the story cute instead of powerful. At a more elemental level, the addition of a vicious movie villain such as Gaston keeps us from realizing that in the fairy tale, Beauty becomes the real villain by abandoning the Beast, then turns into a hero who saves him from loneliness. A few scenes in the Disney film do focus on the love between Beauty and the Beast: the dance scene between the two, for instance, is true to the fairy tale and deeply touching. The clatter of teacups quiets so we can hear the heartbeat of the story.

Whatever the Disney film of Beauty and the Beast—or of Cinderella or of Snow White—says about our culture, it's important to seek out and stay open to other versions. Simply knowing that there *are* different versions paves the way for making choices. In a dark movie theater, teacups may seem like fun, but they're not much company on a dark journey. There you need the power to make your own way.

Activities

The following activities can be adapted to children of various ages. I have used the first question below—"What stories have you heard today?"—with both first-graders and college seniors. In fact, the graduate students in my oral narrative classes all keep story diaries, an exercise I've also seen successfully used for folklore units in the elementary grades. Each section is based on a type of activity: awareness and collection of stories, literary analysis, storytelling, cultural comparison, discussion of social values, drama, music, film and video, art, and writing. The more creative the activity, the more creative the child's response will be.

● Stories are a way of life. You are surrounded by stories from morning till night. You hear them on TV or radio, at school or work, in the house or on the street. Stories appear as jokes, songs, and anecdotes as well as fables, myths, and fairy tales. What stories have you heard today? What stories could you tell about the saddest or happiest or most embarrassing events in your life? Do some of those stories get told over and over to become part of your family "mythology"? (Instead of "Once upon a time," such stories often start out "Do you remember the time when . . . ?") What do these stories tell about you and your family?

● Keep a story diary for a week. You can retell stories that you've heard from friends and family, or stories you've overheard on the bus or playground. At the end of the week, see if you can identify some heroes and villains in the stories you've written down, some conflicts and resolutions.

Notice how the best stories have a strong beginning, middle, and end—they don't just wander around and fizzle out. Somebody doing one thing causes another thing to happen, which causes another thing to happen.

● Pick several entries from your story diary and analyze them by making a list of the characters, incidents, and objects in each one. You are starting to identify motifs, or recurring characters and incidents. Do any of the stories repeat basic kinds of actions and characters? Can you observe any plot or character patterns in the way these motifs fit together?

● Read another book of folktales or fairy tales or myths. These are stories that have already been shaped for smooth telling by thousands of people over hundreds of years. The plots and characters have become a kind of code. A motif may appear in several different stories. Make a list of the stories you like best. Do they have similar motifs or themes? Are they funny, sad, romantic, tricky?

● Pick out your favorite folktale, fairy tale, or myth and read it through several times. Put the book away, close your eyes, and run the story through your mind as if it were a movie you were watching. Notice the details you imagine about the way the characters look and talk to each other, what the house or landscape looks like, and how the action unfolds. Take time to see all these things in your mind's eye. Now go and tell the story to a friend. Tell it to another friend. Tell it to your family. Tell it to anyone who will listen. If everyone's tired of listening, tell it to a mirror (the hardest task of all). Notice how you make up new bits while you're telling the story and then incorporate those bits the next time you tell it. Some things stay the same each time, while other things change. After you've told it a dozen times or so, go back and read the "original" again. You've probably kept all the important parts but added or subtracted details. You've made it yours. Since no two people are alike, no one will tell that story exactly the way you do unless he or she memorizes it out of the book, which is boring to do and boring to hear.

● When you pass on a story you've heard, you have joined the oral tradition and started to cultivate a style of your own. Using the same techniques you developed to learn your favorite folk or fairy tale, pick out and learn another very brief story. Form a circle with some of your friends. Whisper the story to the one nearest you and have him or her do the same to the next person until the story has gone all around. Then have the last person tell his or her version and compare it with your own. What are the differences? The similarities?

● Reading the stories in this book will make you familiar with the basic story elements in several related tale types. Though the details of the stories change with each telling, the basic story elements often remain the same. Compare the stories "Cupid and Psyche" and "Beauty and the Beast." Can you see similarities between the sets of characters in each story? What are the differences in the two plots?

● Both of these stories send messages about the nature of love. Although Psyche and Beauty both learn to love, they do it in different ways. Pick out another story and see if the heroine's tests are physical, like Psyche's, or emotional, like Beauty's. Do you see any cultural values or rules of moral conduct implied in the tests that various Beauties must undergo?

● Just as every person tells a story differently, every person also hears a different story. What you hear depends on your background, experience, and culture. Because you respond to different aspects of a story, or respond to the same aspects differently, you will find your own meaning in the story. No two listeners interpret a story in exactly the same way. The amazing thing about stories is how many different meanings they can hold. A story is your own to think about and live with. No one can take it away from you. A story can grow deeper, however, if you ask yourself private questions about it. (Have you ever felt like a Beauty, a Beast, or maybe both?) If you're comfortable with a small group, you can also discuss questions about the story with other listeners. (Have they discovered any individuals who seemed scary on the outside but who were really warmhearted once you got to know them?) Do you think any of these stories generate ethical or moral questions about the character's actions? Select a set of characters and try to imagine that they decided on a different course of action from the one they took in the story. How might these alternative choices have changed the characters' lives and the ending of the story you're focusing on?

● Through role playing, story theater, and creative dramatics you can explore a story's meanings differently from the way you might analyze a story in discussion. Talking a part, or acting it out, is an extension of the storytelling medium. In role playing Beauty and the Beast, for example, two volunteers might pick a scene from the story and improvise a dialogue between the main characters, then swap roles to experience each part. (The scene where Beauty first meets the Beast in his castle is a good example because both of them are so afraid of what will happen next.) A story theater production involves a narrator's telling or reading "Beauty and the Beast" with others pantomiming the action. Creative dramatics would mean a fuller treatment of the story in which a whole cast of characters acts out the plot with extemporized dialogue. Although no props or scripts are required, the actors must have internalized the story to the extent of spontaneously developing their roles through smoothly coordinated scenes. Of course, any one of these stories could make an elaborate play, with intriguing possibilities for lighting, stage backdrops, costumes, and formal parts just waiting to be organized by an energetic director. For a smaller cast, choose a simple story such as "The Dough Prince"; to include a whole class, reach for more complex versions such as "The Singing, Soaring Lark."

● Mime, dance, and music can express a story in dynamic terms of movement and sound. "Beauty and the Beast" has inspired several ballets and operas. Music, in fact, was the most outstanding aspect of Disney's "Beauty and the Beast." Since operas and film scores are beyond the scope of most beginners, start with the instrument you play and experiment with some notes that summon the mood of the story you know best. After a while, you'll find a musical motif—a melody or sequence of notes—that you like to play over and over, the more haunting the better. That musical motif is the start of a song, with or without words. If you're more physical than musical, try expressing the story in movement.

Based on the assumption that the audience is familiar with the plot and characters, you can mime or dance all the parts or, with the help of others, choreograph your own jazz or ballet production. The single-character mime can be more spontaneous, of course, since assembling any group requires planning and rehearsal. However, classes or groups that are used to working together and have an experienced leader can handle the challenge of choreography as capably as they can a verbal or theatrical exercise.

● It's important for every one of us to become film, video, and television critics. These media are primary sources of entertainment and information for millions of people, especially children. Stories are shaped and reshaped when you see and hear them at the movies or on television. "Beauty and the Beast" and its variants have gotten much media attention, both directly and indirectly. It's up to you to decide what that attention has done to the story and what you think of the results. Some of the versions come and go, never to reappear, such as the television series "Beauty and the Beast." It got high popularity ratings for a while, then changed direction from a fairy tale to a cops-and-robbers vengeance story and disappeared forever. Films are more long lasting. In fact, some of them have more impact than they should. Many viewers will never hear a version of Beauty and the Beast other than the one Disney studios released in 1991. Write down the characters in the film and list the incidents that make up the plot. Then write down the characters and incidents in the story as it appears in this book. What are the differences? What difference do they make? Watch Jean Cocteau's classic film from 1946, and compare it to the Disney version. (Both films have added an important character, but he affects the story differently.) Look at Shelley Duvall's Story Theater version of "Beauty and the Beast." How does it compare to the longer films in terms of script, acting, pace, lighting, music, and special effects? Can you think of other films that have elements of the Beauty and the Beast story, such as *Edward Scissorhands*?

● If you read, you qualify as a book critic. One of the most satisfying experiences of any reader is to connect with another person who has enjoyed the same book and who gets excited talking about it. You can make this a regular thing by starting a reading group of a few friends who enjoy reading the same kinds of books. Beauty and Beast stories are a good starting point because the motifs have inspired so many authors and artists. If you're into fantasy, try Robin McKinley's novel *Beauty* or Tanith Lee's science fiction novella *Beauty* for a futuristic version. You can also read and compare the narrative and pictorial styles of the following picture books, which incorporate the art of illustration into telling the story: *Beauty and the Beast* by Marianna Mayer, illustrations by Mercer Mayer (Four Winds Press, 1978); *Beauty and the Beast*, adapted and illustrated by Warwick Hutton (Macmillan/McElderry Books, 1985); *Beauty and the Beast*, illustrated by Etienne Delessert (Creative Education, 1984); and *Beauty and the Beast* by Nancy Willard, illustrated by Barry Moser (Harcourt, 1992). Take a look at *Mufaro's Beautiful Daughters: An African Tale*, illustrated by John Steptoe (Lothrop, 1987), and compare it to "The Story of Five Heads," the African version of the tale in this book. (Both this version and Steptoe's were adapted from the same source.) Read Paul Goble's *Buffalo Woman*

(Bradbury, 1984) and see what elements of a Beauty and the Beast tale you find there.

● Now that you've looked at several artists' ideas of Beauties and Beasts, draw or paint your own. Your art doesn't have to look like or "be as good as" anyone else's; in fact, it can consist of line or color impressions. Just stretch your imagination as far as it will go. If you like your characters, draw or paint them through the story. You can bind a series of pictures into a wordless picture book or write your own version of a Beauty and the Beast story—medieval, modern, or futuristic—to go with your illustrations.

● Sometimes the best way to understand a story is to write about it—not a book report, but a *response* to the story. You can pick a character you like and write about him or her, or you can describe a castle or a magic object in detail. You can write a poem from the point of view of one of the characters. The poem could be narrative, a rhythmic retelling of the story that may or may not rhyme (reread the two ballads in this book), or lyric, expressing reactions to or emotions connected with a story.

● One of the best ways to keep a story is to pass it on. That may sound contradictory, but when you tell the story to someone else, you make it your own in a unique way. Bear in mind that the best audiences are sometimes the youngest. Brothers, sisters, and kids in younger classes at school make ideal listeners, whether they're in a group setting or in the bed next to yours after the lights have been turned out. Even whispered, the story has a life of its own.

Some Picture Book Versions of Beauty and the Beast

This recommend list, while it does show a range and variety of *Beauty and the Beast* picture book editions, is subject to constant change as books go into and out of print. The selection of anyone's favorite version depends partly on what's available in libraries or bookstores and partly on individual taste. Take some time to look at and read the editions you can find. Using this bibliography as a starting point, you will ultimately want to make your own list, help students observe the differences in artistic interpretation of the same story, and encourage them to make their own picture book versions.

Apy, Deborah. *Beauty and the Beast*. Illustrated by Michael Hague. New York: Holt, Rinehart and Winston, 1983.
>   A long version that incorporates complicated elements into both story and art, this book features paintings heavily influenced by Arthur Rackham and a text reflective of Jean Cocteau's film script.

Beauty and the Beast. Illustrations selected and arranged by Cooper Edens. San Diego: The Green Tiger Press, 1989.
>   A nineteenth-century retelling illustrated with pictures from a variety of artists, including Edmund Dulac, Walter Crane, Margaret Evans Price, Eleanor Vere Boyle, Arthur Rackham, and others—all well reproduced and interesting from a historical point of view.

Carter, Anne. *Beauty and the Beast*. Illustrated by Binette Schroeder. New York: Potter/Crown, 1986.
>   Mannered paintings, with characters posed in operatic costume and posture, illustrate a close adaptation of Beaumont's fairy tale.

Gerstein, Mordicai. *Beauty and the Beast*. New York: Dutton, 1989.
>   Ornate pen drawings in subdued clay tones accompany this informal version.

Harris, Rosemary. *Beauty and the Beast*. Illustrated by Errol LeCain. New York: Doubleday, 1980.
>   A highly patterned, stylized series of paintings elaborates on Harris's competent retelling.

Hutton, Warwick. *Beauty and the Beast*. New York: Margaret K. McElderry Books, 1985.
>   Hutton resists over-romanticizing the story in favor of crisp art with sharp contrasts between dark and light and with interesting perspectives that show insight into the story, pared down here for smooth reading aloud.

Jones, Olive, ed. *Beauty and the Beast*. Little Box of Fairy Tales, illustrated by Francesca Crespi. New York: Dial, 1983.
>   The distinction of this set is its small size and miniature art work, which children who like handsize books will find attractive.

Knight, Hilary. *Beauty and the Beast*. New York: Simon and Schuster, 1990.
>   A Disney-like cast, elongated for an Art Deco look, gets bright-colored treatment in this translation by a noted poet.

Le Prince de Beaumont, Madame. *Beauty and the Beast*. Translated and illustrated by Diane Goode. Scarsdale, New York: Bradbury Press, 1978.
>   Goode's rather flowery art, flavored with French Court elegance, accompanies her own translation of Madame Le Prince de Beaumont' story.

Mayer, Marianna. *Beauty and the Beast*. Illustrated by Mercer Mayer. New York: Four Winds Press, 1978.
>   A dramatic retelling especially suited for reading aloud to younger children, this is illustrated with dynamic paintings that keep the pages turning almost as quickly as a film, yet give each viewer plenty of Gothic detail to linger over.

Osborne, Mary Pope. *Beauty and the Beast.* Illustrated by Winslow Pinney Pels. New York: Scholastic, 1987
  Pels' figures have a sculptured effect that is more graceful than the text, which is best suited to a preschool audience because of the abbreviation of story and simplification of style.

Pearce, Philippa. *Beauty and the Beast.* Illustrated by Alan Barrett. New York: Thomas Y. Crowell, 1972.
  Powerful, impressionistic paintings project a brooding tone over this spare adaptation.

Villeneuve, Gabrielle Susanne Barbot de Gallon (Madame) de. *Beauty and the Beast.* Illustrated by Etienne Delessert. Mankato, MN: Creative Education Inc., 1984.
  A sophisticated book with surrealistic paintings that plumb the symbolic levels of the story, this has been retold from Villeneuve's 1740 version, which was even earlier than Beaumont's.

Willard, Nancy. *Beauty and the Beast.* Illustrated by Barry Moser. San Diego: Harcourt, Brace, Jovanovich, 1992.
  Set in New York early in the twentieth century, this has been developed with fictional characters, an elaborate setting, and stark black-and-white wood engravings that project a dark American Gothic aura.

Some Related Tales of Transformation in Picture Book Form

Aksadov, Sergei. *The Scarlet Flower: A Russian Folk Tale.* Translated by Isadora Levin. Illustrated by Boris Diodorov. San Diego: Harcourt, Brace, Jovanovich, 1989.
  A long, nineteenth-century Russian variant of "Beauty and the Beast," this features traditionally costumed characters in elaborate scenes.

Barth, Edna. *Cupid and Psyche: A Love Story.* Illustrated by Ati Forberg. Boston: Houghton Mifflin, 1979.
  Wash drawings in black, white, and rust incorporate Grecian motifs to accompany this mythical love story.

Berenzy, Alix. *The Frog Prince.* New York: Henry Holt, 1989.
  With nuance of line and rich color, Berenzy illustrates a story that she has rewritten for a surprise ending: the frog finds a sleeping frog

princess and the two live happily ever after, content with their own amphibian selves.

Cooney, Barbara, illus. *Snow White and Rose Red.* New York: Delacorte, 1991.
  A simplified retelling of the Grimm tale about two sisters and an enchanted bear has illustrations that are sweet without becoming sentimental.

Cooper, Susan, ad. *The Selkie Girl.* Illustrated by Warwick Hutton. New York: Margaret K. McElderry Books, 1986.
  A lonely fisherman falls in love with a beautiful seal maiden, hiding her seal skin so she cannot return to the sea; cool blue watercolors and rhythmic prose grace this ancient Celtic legend.

Dasent, George W. *East o' the Sun and West o' the Moon.* Illustrated by Gillian Barlow. New York: Putnam/Philomel, 1988.
  The soft tones and rounded shapes of Barlow's full-color illustrations are set off by elegant borders to complement this story of the girl who journeys so far to recover her true love, first from his bear shape and then from a troll bride.

Dasent, George W. *East O' the Sun and West O' the Moon.* Illus. by P. J. Lynch. Cambridge, MA: Candlewick Press, 1992.
  Glamorous paintings, especially literal in detailing the ugly Troll folk who hold captive the heroine's betrothed, dramatize Dasent's lilting translation of the Norwegian classic.

Gerstein, Mordicai, ad. *The Seal Mother.* New York: Dial, 1986.
  Dancing shapes within square-framed compositions extend Gerstein's animated adaptation of the Selkie tale.

Goble, Paul. *Buffalo Woman.* Scarsdale, New York: Bradbury Press, 1984.
  Based on several versions of a Plains Indian tale, this recounts a warrior's search for his buffalo wife and son, but in this ending, the human is transformed into an animal, as Goble depicts in his stylized paintings.

Goble, Paul. *The Girl Who Loved Wild Horses.* Scarsdale, New York: Bradbury Press, 1978.
  This Native American story portrays a beauty transformed into what she finds most beautiful, a horse; Goble's illustrations won the Caldecott Award in 1979.

Hastings, Selina, ed. *Sir Gawain and the Loathly Lady.* Illustrated by Juan Wijngaard. New York: Lothrop, 1985.
  Jewel-toned paintings create a medieval setting

for Hastings' solid retelling of the ugly bride who wins her way, along with Sir Gawain's heart.

Hodges, Margaret. *The Arrow and the Lamp: The Story of Psyche*. Illustrated by Donna Diamond. Boston: Little Brown, 1989.
   Although the art work for this version of "Cupid and Psyche" has an over-glamorized Hollywood quality, the story is well adapted, and the picture book may have appeal for diehard romantics.

Lewis, Naomi, tr. *The Frog Prince*. Illustrated by Binette Schroeder. New York: North-South Books, 1989.
   With a nice balance between formal and colloquial language, Lewis provides a readable text for Schroeder's intense pictorial sequences, which are appropriately steeped in green.

Lloyd, David. *The Frog Prince*. Illustrated by Jan Ormerod. New York: Lothrop, 1990.
   Wistfully humorous watercolors framed with delicate motifs enhance a lyrical adaptation of the Grimm tale.

San Souci, Robert D. *The White Cat*. Illustrated by Gennady Spirin. New York: Orchard/Watts, 1990.
   Gold-toned paintings embellishing scenes of courtly grandeur accompany this long text based on Madame D'Aulnoy's 1698 literary tale, wherein love transforms—into a human bride—the magical white cat who has helped a prince pass three tests that determine his inheritance.

Scieszka, Jon. *The Frog Prince, Continued*. Illustrated by Steve Johnson. New York: Viking Press, 1991.

Students will laugh at Scieszka's satire, one of many based on this traditional Grimm tale; here, the transformation from frog to prince is neither total nor totally happy until a second, rather unexpected transformation takes place, and it's all shown with bug-eyed irreverence in Johnson's dark-hued art.

Steptoe, John. *Mufaro's Beautiful Daughters: An African Tale*. New York: Lothrop, 1987.
   Large-scale paintings follow the fortunes of two African sisters, one jealous and the other so pure in heart that she wins a prince, who has appeared to her as a green garden snake.

Tarcov, Edith, ad. *The Frog Prince*. Illustrated by James Marshall. New York: Scholastic, 1987.
   The text is traditional, but the art is comical, with Marshall's characteristic flair for drawing animals in the funniest possible poses.

Watts, Bernadette, illus. *Snow White and Rose Red*. New York: North-South Books, 1988.
   An oversize format gives full play to russet pictures accompanying the Grimms' tale of two good sisters who free a prince from his enchantment as a bear.

Willard, Nancy. *East of the Sun and West of the Moon*. Illustrated by Barry Moser. San Diego: Harcourt, 1989.
   With lilting rhythms and rhymes, Willard has adapted this story into a memorable play in verse form; Moser's watercolor portraits are astute, with occasional scenes lit like a stage backdrop.

Sources

"Beauty and the Beast" from *Magasin des enfans* [sic], *ou dialogues entre une sage gouvernante et plusiers de ses élèves de la premiére distinction* (*The Young Misses Magazine, containing Dialogues between a Governess and Several Young Ladies of Quality her Scholars*) by Madame Le Prince de Beaumont (London: J. Haberkorn, 1756). Translated by Howard Batchelor. [French]

"The Enchanted Tsarevitch" from *Russian Folk-Tales* by Aleksandr Nikolaevich Afanas'ev (London: Kegan Paul, Trench, Trubner; New York: E. P. Dutton, republished by Gale Research, Detroit, 1974), pp. 283-86. [Russian]

"The Princess and the Pig" from *A Treasury of Turkish Folktales* by Barbara Walker (Hamden, CT: Linnet Books, 1988), pp. 114-17. [Turkish]

"A Bunch of Laurel Blooms for a Present" from *Tales from the Cloud Walking Country* by Marie Campbell (Bloomington: Indiana University Press, 1958), pp. 228-30. [Appalachian]

"The Small-Tooth Dog" from *Folktales of England* ed. by Katharine M. Briggs and Ruth L. Tongue (Chicago: University of Chicago Press, 1965), pp. 3-5. [English]

"The Fairy Serpent" from *Chinese Fairy Tales* by A. M. Fielde (New York: Putnam, 1893), pp. 45-51. [Chinese]

"The Monkey Son-in-law" from *Ancient Tales in Modern Japan: An Anthology of Japanese Folk Tales* selected and edited by Fanny Hagin Mayer (Bloomington: Indiana University Press, 1984), pp. 41-43. [Japanese]

"The Lizard Husband" from *Oceanic Mythology*, vol. IX of *The Mythology of All Races* ed. by Louis Herbert Gray (Boston: Marshall Jones, 1916), pp. 210-13. [Indonesian]

"Cupid and Psyche" from *Metamorphases, Book 11* by Apuleius, ed. by J. Gwyn Griffiths. (Leiden: E.J. Brill, 1975). Translated by Howard Batchelor. [Greco-Roman]

"The Serpent and the Grape-Grower's Daughter" from *French Fairy Tales* by Paul Delarue (New York: Knopf, 1968), pp. 104-09 (story collected in 1893). [French]

"The Singing, Soaring Lark" from *Grimms' Household Tales* tr. by Margaret Hunt (London: George Bill and Sons, 1844), pp. 5-10. [German]

"East of the Sun and West of the Moon" from *Popular Tales from the Norse* by Peter Christen Asbjørnsen and Jørgen Moe (Edinburgh: David Douglas, 1888, republished by Dover Publications, New York, 1970), pp. 22-35. [Scandanavian]

"Whitebear Whittington" from *Grandfather Tales* ed. by Richard Chase (Boston: Houghton Mifflin, 1948), pp. 52-64. [Appalachian]

"The Three Daughters of King O'Hara" from *Myths and Folk-Lore of Ireland* by Jeremiah Curtin (Boston: Little, Brown & Co., 1906), pp. 50-63. [Irish]

"The Black Bull of Norroway" from *More English Fairy Tales* by Joseph Jacobs (New York: Putnam's, 1895), pp. 344-48. [Scottish]

"Bull-of-all-the-Land" in *Jamaica Anansi Stories* by Martha Warren Beckwith (New York: The American Folk-Lore Society, 1924), pp. 130-31. [Jamaican]

"Prince White Hog" from *It's Good to Tell You* by Rosemary Hyde Thomas (Columbia: University of Missouri Press, 1981), pp. 66-75. [Missouri French]

"The Enchanted Prince" from *The Folklore of Spain in the American Southwest* by Aurelio M. Espinosa (Norman: University of Oklahoma Press, 1985), pp. 191-95. [Spanish American]

"The Story of Five Heads" from *Kaffir Folk-Lore* by George McCall Theal (London: W. Swan Sonnenschein, 1882), pp. 47-53. [African]

"The Ten Serpents" from *Folktales of Israel* ed. by Dov Noy (Chicago: University of Chicago Press, 1963), pp. 161-65. [Israeli]

"Egle, Queen of Serpents" from *Lietuviu Tautosaka*, vol. 3, ed. by Lietuviu Kalbos Ir Literaturos Institutas (Vilnius: Lietuvos TSR Mokslu Akademija, 1965), pp. 296-300. [Lithuanian]

"Old Man Coyote, the Young Man and Two Otter Sisters" from "Traditions of the Crows" by S.C. Simms, in *Field Columbian Museum Publication 85 Anthropological Series 2:6* (October, 1903), pp. 297-99. [Native American]

"The Laidley Worm of Spindleston Heughs" and "Kemp Owyne" from *The English and Scottish Popular*

Ballads ed. by Francis James Child, vol. 1 (New York: Dover Publications, 1965), pp.309, 312-13. [Scottish]

"Sir Gawain and the Loathly Lady" adapted by Joanna Hearne from "The Weddynge of Sir Gawen and Dame Ragnell" published and edited by Laura Sumner from a rotographic copy of MS. Rawlinson C. 86 in the Bodleian Library. In *Smith College Studies in Modern Languages* 5:4 (July, 1924), pp. 1-24. [English]

"Pinto Smalto" from *The Pentamerone of Giambattista Basile* tr. from the Italian of Benedetto Croce (London: John Lane the Bodley Head (1932); New York: Dutton, 1932), pp. 114-18. [Italian]

"The Dough Prince" from *The Green Hills of Magic: West Virginia Folktales from Europe* by Ruth Ann Musick (Lexington: University Press of Kentucy, 1970), pp. 149-51. [Appalachian]

Bibliography

A comprehensive listing of variants related to the several tale types included in this anthology would be a book unto itself. The following bibliography includes some variants I liked but couldn't fit into this volume and a number of collections that storytellers will find useful. Books published for children are marked with an asterisk. The second half of the bibliography comprises critical sources that were valuable in collecting and considering the stories.

Stories

Afanas'ev, Aleksandr Nikolaevich. "The Feather of Finist, the Bright Falcon." In *Russian Folk-Tales*. London: Kegan Paul, Trench, Trubner; New York: E. P. Dutton, republished by Gale Research, Detroit, 1974.

Apuleius. *Cupid and Psyche and Other Tales from The Golden Ass of Aurelius*. Edited by W. H. D. Rouse. London: Chatto and Windus, 1907.

————. *The Most Pleasant and Delectable Tale of the Marriage of Cupid and Psyche, Done into English by William Adlington of University College in Oxford, with a Discourse on the Fable by Andrew Lang, Late of Merton College in Oxford*. London: David Nutt, 1887.

Arnott, Kathleen. "The Snake Chief." In *African Myths and Legends*. London: Oxford University Press, 1962.

Asbjørnsen, Peter Christen and Jørgen Moe. *Popular Tales from the Norse*. Edinburgh: David Douglas, 1888.

Barchers, Suzanne, ed. *Wise Women: Folk and Fairy Tales from around the World*. New York: Libraries Unlimited, 1990.

Basile, Giambattista. *The Pentamerone of Giambattista Basile, translated from the Italian of Benedetto Croce*. By N. M. Penzer. Vol. 1. New York and London: E. P. Dutton, 1932.

Beaumont. See Le Prince de Beaumont, Madame.

Beauty and the Beast Ballet. An ABC Films release, 1966. Produced by Gordon Waldear. Featuring the San Francisco Ballet, music by Tchaikovsky, choreography by Lew Christensen, narration by Haley Mills. With Robert Gladstein, Lynda Meyer, David Anderson. Color, 50 minutes.

Beauty and the Beast. Produced by Shelley Duvall. A Faerie Tale Theatre Production, 1984.

Beckwith, Martha W. *Jamaica Anansi Stories*. New York: The American Folk-Lore Society, 1924.

Boas, Franz. "The Sold Child" from "Tales of Spanish Provenience from Zuni" from *Journal of American Folk-Lore* 35: 66-73. New York: The American Folk-Lore Society, 1922.

Briggs, Katharine and Ruth L. Tongue. *Folktales from England*. Chicago: University of Chicago Press, 1965.

Calvino, Italo. "Belinda and the Monster." In *Italian Folktales*. Translated by George Martin. New York: Harcourt, Brace, Jovanovich, 1980.

Campbell, Marie. "The Girl That Married a Flop-Eared Hound-Dog." In *Tales from the Cloud Walking Country*. Bloomington: University of Indiana Press, 1958.

Carter, Angela, "The Courtship of Mr. Lyon." In *Elsewhere: Tales of Fantasy*. 2 vols. Edited by Terri Windling and Mark Alan Arnold. New York: Ace Fantasy, 1982.

*————. *Sleeping Beauty and Other Favourite Fairy Tales*. Translated and edited by Angela Carter. Illustrated by Michael Foreman. North Pomfret, Vt.: Victor Gollancz/David & Charles, 1982.

————, ed. *Old Wives' Fairy Tale Book*. New York: Pantheon, 1990.

*Chase, Richard. *Grandfather Tales*. Cambridge, MA: Houghton Mifflin, 1948.

Child, Francis James, ed. *The English and Scottish Popular Ballads*. Vol. 1. New York: Dover Publications, 1965; reprint of the 1882 edition.

Clarkson, Atelia and Gilbert B. Cross, eds. *World Folktales: A Scribner Resource Collection*. New York: Scribner's, 1980.

Cocteau, Jean. *Beauty and the Beast*. Film, Paris, 1946.

*Cohen, Barbara. *Roses*. New York: Lothrop, Lee and Shepard Books, 1984.

*Cole, Joanna. *Best-loved Folktales of the World*. New York: Doubleday, 1982.

Colum, Padraic. *Storytelling, New and Old*. New York: Macmillan, 1968.

Colwell, Eileen. *A Storyteller's Choice*. New York: Walck, 1964.

Cook, Elizabeth. *The Ordinary and the Fabulous: An Introduction to Myths, Legends and Fairy Tales for Teachers and Storytellers*. 2nd ed. New York: Cambridge University Press, 2nd ed., 1975.

Cowell, E. B. *The Jataka, or, Stories of the Buddha's Former Births: Translated from the Pali by Various Hands*. Vol. 5. Reprint. London: Luzac, 1969.

*Crane, Walter. *Beauty and the Beast and Other Tales*. London: Thames and Hudson, 1982.

Curtin, Jeremiah. *Myths and Folk-Lore of Ireland*. Boston: Little, Brown & Co., 1906.

———. "Sgiathán Dearg and the Daughter of the King of the Western World." In *Irish Folk-Tales*. Edited with introduction and notes by Séamus O'Duilearga. Dublin: Folklore of Ireland Society, 1943.

———, trans. *Myths and Folk-tales of the Russians, Western Slavs, and Magyars*. Boston: Little, Brown & Co., 1890.

Dawkins, R. M., ed. and trans. "Cupid and Psyche" or "The Crab" from *Modern Greek Folktales* selected and translated by R. M. Dawkins. Westport, CT: Greenwood Press, 1974; reprint, Oxford: Clarendon Press, 1953.

*Delarue, Paul. *French Fairy Tales*. New York: Knopf, 1968.

Dorson, Richard. "The Seven Young Sky Women." In *Folktales Told around the World*. Chicago: University of Chicago Press, 1975.

Espinosa, Aurelio M. *The Folklore of Spain in the American Southwest*. Norman: University of Oklahoma Press, 1985.

*Fielde, A. M. *Chinese Fairy Tales*. New York: Putnam, 1893.

Grimm, Jakob Ludwig Karl and Wilhelm Karl Grimm. *Grimms' Tales for Young and Old: The Complete Stories*. Translated by Ralph Manheim. New York: Doubleday, 1977.

Grinnell, George Bird. "The Buffalo Wife." In *By Cheyenne Campfires*. New Haven: Yale University Press, 1926.

*Halfyard, Lynda and Karen Rose. *Kristin and Boone*. Boston: Houghton Mifflin, 1983.

*Haviland, Virginia. *Favorite Fairy Tales Told in France*. Illustrated by Roger Duvoisin. Boston: Little, Brown & Co., 1959.

*Holme, Bryan, ed. *Tales from Times Past*. New York: Viking Press, 1977.

*Jacobs, Joseph. "The Laidley Worm of Spindleston Heughs." In *English Fairy Tales*. New York: G. P. Putnam's, 1892.

Kinsley, James, ed. "King Henry." In *The Oxford Book of Ballads*. New York: Oxford University Press, 1982.

Knappert, Jan. "Monyohe." In *Myths and Legends of Botswana, Lesotho and Swaziland*. Leiden: E. J. Brill, 1985.

*Lang, Andrew. *Blue Fairy Book*. Revised and edited by Brian Alderson from the 1889 edition. New York: Viking, 1975.

*———. *Green Fairy Book*. Revised and edited by Brian Alderson from the 1892 edition. New York: Viking, 1978.

*———. *Red Fairy Book*. Revised and edited by Brian Alderson from the 1890 edition. New York: Viking, 1976.

Le Prince de Beaumont, Madame. *Le magasin des enfans [sic], ou dialogues entre une sage gouvernante et plusiers de ses élèves de la première distinction*. London: J. Haberkorn, 1756.

Lee, Tanith. "Beauty." In *Red as Blood or Tales from the Sisters Grimmer*. New York: Daw Books, 1983.

Lietuviu Kalbos Ir Literaturos Insitutas. *Lietuviu Tautosaka*. Vol. 3. Vilnius: Lietuvos TSR Mokslu Akademija, 1965.

*Lurie, Alison, ed. *Clever Gretchen and Other Forgotten Folktales*. New York: Crowell, 1980.

Mayer, Fanny Hagin. *Ancient Tales in Modern Japan: An Anthology of Japanese Folktales*. Bloomington: Indiana University Press, 1985.

*McKinley, Robin. *Beauty: A Retelling of the Story of Beauty and the Beast*. New York: Harper and Row, 1978.

Mieder, Wolfgang, ed. *Disenchantments: An Anthology of Modern Fairy Tale Poetry.* Hanover, NH: University Press of New England, 1985.

*Minard, Rosemary. *Womenfolk and Fairy Tales.* Boston: Houghton, Mifflin, 1975.

Musick, Ruth Ann. "The Bewitched Princess." In *The Green Hills of Magic: West Virginia Folktales from Europe.* Lexington: University Press of Kentucky, 1970.

Noy, Dov, ed. *Folktales of Israel.* Chicago: University of Chicago Press, 1963.

Opie, Iona and Peter Opie, eds. *The Classic Fairy Tales.* New York: Oxford University Press, 1974.

*Perrault, Charles. *The Glass Slipper: Charles Perrault's Tales of Times Past.* Translated and edited by John Bierhorst. New York: Four Winds Press, 1981.

*Phelps, Ethel Johnston. *The Maid of the North: Feminist Folk Tales from around the World.* Illustrated by Lloyd Bloom. New York: Holt, Rinehart and Winston, 1981.

*Provensen, Alice and Martin Provensen. *The Provensen Book of Fairy Tales.* New York: Random House, 1971.

Ralston, W. R. S. *Tibetan Tales Derived from Indian Sources: Translated from the Tibetan of the Kah-Gyur by F. Anton von Schiefner, done into English from the German.* London, 1893.

*Riordan, James. *The Woman in the Moon and Other Tales of Forgotten Heroines.* New York: Dial, 1985.

Roberts, Leonard W. "Bully Bornes" and "The Enchanted Cat." In *South from Hell-fer-Sartin.* Berea, KY: The Council of Southern Mountains, 1964.

Schimmel, Nancy. *Just Enough to Make a Story: A Sourcebook for Storytelling.* Rev. ed. Berkeley: Sisters' Choice Press, 1992.

Seki, Keigo, ed. *Folktales of Japan.* Chicago: University of Chicago Press, 1963.

Sexton, Anne. *Transformations.* Boston: Houghton, Mifflin, 1971.

*Shannon, George. *The Oryx Multicultural Folktale Series: A Knock at the Door.* Phoenix, AZ: Oryx Press, 1992.

Sietel, Peter. "The Serpent of Kam Ushalanga." As told by Ma Kelezensia Konstantin in *See So That We May See: Performances and Interpretations of Traditional Tales from Tanzania.* From performances tape recorded by Sheila Dauer and Peter Seitel. Bloomington: Indiana University Press, 1980.

*Sierra, Judy. *The Oryx Multicultural Folktale Series: Cinderella.* Phoenix, AZ: Oryx Press, 1992.

Simms, S. C. "Traditions of the Crows." In *Field Columbian Museum Publication 85 Anthropological series* vol. 2:6 (October, 1903).

Sumner, Laura, ed. "The Weddynge of Sir Gawen and Dame Ragnell." *Smith College Studies in Modern Languages* vol. 5:4 (July, 1924).

Sutherland, Zena and Myra Cohn Livingston. *The Scott Foresman Anthology of Children's Literature.* Glenview, IL: Scott Foresman, 1984.

Theal, George McCall. "The Story of the Bird That Made Milk." In *Kaffir Folk-lore, or, A Selection from the Traditional Tales Current among the People Living on the Eastern Border of the Cape Colony.* London: W. Swan Sonnenschein, 1882.

Thomas, Rosemary Hyde. *It's Good To Tell You: French Folktales from Missouri.* Columbia: University of Missouri Press, 1981.

*Walker, Barbara. *A Treasury of Turkish Folktales for Children.* Hamden, CT: Linnet Books, 1988.

Williamson, Duncan, ed. "The Hedgehurst." In *Fireside Tales of the Traveler Children: Twelve Scottish Tales.* New York: Harmony Books, 1985.

Zipes, Jack. *Beauties, Beasts, and Enchantment: Classic French Fairytales.* New York: Penguin, 1989.

———. *Don't Bet on the Prince: Contemporary Feminist Fairy Tales in North America and England.* London: Methuen, 1986.

Criticism

Aarne, Antti. *The Types of the Folktale: A Classification and Bibliography.* Translated and revised by Stith Thompson. Folklore Fellows Communications, no. 184. Helsinki: Academia Scientiarum Fennica, 1961.

Ashliman, D. L. *A Guide to Folktales in the English Language: Based on the Aarne-Thompson Classification System.* Westport, CT: Greenwood Press, 1987.

Baker, Augusta and Ellin Greene. *Storytelling: Art and Technique.* Bowker, 1977.

Barchilon, Jacques. "Beauty and the Beast." *Modern Language Review* 56 (1961): 81–82.

———. "Beauty and the Beast: From Myth To Fairy Tale," *Psychoanalysis and the Psychoanalytic Review* 46 no. 4 (Winter, 1959): 19–29.

Bauer, Caroline Feller. *Handbook for Storytellers.* American Library Association, 1977.

Bauman, Richard. *Story, Performance, and Event: Contextual Studies of Oral Narrative.* New York: Cambridge University Press, 1986.

———. *Verbal Art as Performance.* Rowley, MA: Newbury House, 1977.

Bettelheim, Bruno. *The Uses of Enchantment: The Meaning and Importance of Fairy Tales.* New York: Random House/Vintage, 1977.

Bottigheimer, Ruth. *Grimms' Bad Girls and Bold Boys: The Moral and Social Vision of the Tales.* New Haven: Yale University Press, 1987.

———, ed. *Fairy Tales and Society: Illusion, Allusion, and Paradigm.* Philadelphia: University of Pennsylvania Press, 1986.

Brewer, Derek. "The Battleground of Home: Versions of Fairy Tales." *Encounter* (April 1980): 52–61.

Briggs, Katharine M. *A Dictionary of British Folk-Tales in the English Language.* 2 vols. Bloomington: Indiana University Press, 1970.

Campbell, Joseph. *The Hero with a Thousand Faces.* Princeton: Princeton University Press, 1973.

———. *The Way of the Animal Powers.* Vol. 1 of *The Historical Atlas of World Mythology.* New York: Harper and Row, 1984.

Canham, Stephen. "What Manner of Beast? Illustrations of 'Beauty and the Beast.'" In *Image & Maker: An Annual Dedicated to the Consideration of Book Illustration.* Edited by Harold Darling and Peter Neumeyer. La Jolla, CA: GreenTiger Press, 1984.

Darnton, Robert. *The Great Cat Massacre and Other Episodes in French Cultural History.* New York: Basic Books, 1984.

De George, Richard and Fernande De George, eds. *The Structuralists from Marx to Lévi-Strauss.* Garden City, NY: Doubleday/Anchor Books, 1972.

Degh, Linda. *Folktales and Society: Storytelling in a Hungarian Peasant Community.* Bloomington: Indiana University Press, 1989.

Delarue, Paul and Marie-Louise Tenèze. *Le conte populaire français: Catalogue raisonné des versions de France et des pays de langue française d'outre-mer; Canada, Louisiane, ilots française des Etats-Unis, Antilles françaises, Haïti, Ile Maurice, La Réunion.* Vol. 2. Paris: Éditions G.-P. Maisonneuve et Larose, 1964.

Dixon, Roland B. *The Mythology of All Races: In Thirteen Volumes. Vol. 9. Oceanic.* Boston: Marshall Jones, 1916.

Dorson, Richard. *Handbook of American Folklore.* Bloomington: Indiana University Press, 1983.

———, ed. *Folklore and Folklife: An Introduction.* Chicago: University of Chicago Press, 1972.

Dundes, Alan. *The Morphology of North American Indian Folktales,* Folklore Fellows Communications, no. 195. Helsinki: Suomalainen Tiedeakatemia, 1964.

———, ed. *The Study of Folklore.* Englewood Cliffs, NJ: Prentice-Hall, 1965.

Durand, Gilbert. "Psyche's View," *Spring* (1981): 1-19.

Eastman, Mary. *Index to Fairy Tales, Myths, and Legends.* Boston: F. W. Faxon, 1926, 1937, 1952.

Ellis, John M. *One Fairy Story Too Many.* Chicago: University of Chicago Press, 1983.

Favat, André. *Child and Tale: The Origins of Interest.* No. 19 in a series of research reports sponsored by the NCTE Committee on Research. Urbana, IL: National Council of Teachers of English, 1977.

Freud, Sigmund. "Fairy Tale Subjects in Dreams." In *Collected Papers.* Vol. 4. New York: International Psycho-analytical Press, 1924–1925.

———. *On Creativity and the Unconscious: Papers on the Psychology of Art, Literature, Love, Religion.* Edited by Benjamin Nelson. New York: Harper and Row, 1958.

Fromm, Erich. *The Forgotten Language: An Introduction to the Understanding of Dreams, Fairy Tales, and Myths.* New York: Holt, Rinehart, and Winston, 1951.

Funk and Wagnalls Standard Dictionary of Folklore, Myth, and Legend. New York: Funk and Wagnalls Co., 1949.

Gardner, Howard. "Brief on Behalf of Fairy Tales." *Phaedrus: An International Journal of Children's Literature Research* 5 (1978): 14–23.

Glassie, H. *Passing the Time in Ballymenone.* Philadelphia: University of Pennsylvania Press, 1982.

Gose, Elliott. *Mere Creatures: A Study of Modern Fantasy Tales for Children.* Toronto: University of Toronto Press, 1988.

Hallett, Martin and Barbara Karasek, eds. *Folk and Fairy Tales.* New York: Broadview Press, 1991.

*Hamilton, Virginia. "The Known, the Remembered and the Imagined: Celebrating Afro-American Folktales," *Children's Literature in Education* 18, no. 2 (1987): 67-75.

Hearne, Betsy. *Beauty and the Beast: Visions and Revisions of an Old Tale.* Chicago: University of Chicago Press, 1989.

———. "Booking the Brothers Grimm: Art, Adaptations, and Economics." *The Brothers Grimm and Folktale.* Edited. by James M. McGlathery et al. Urbana: University of Illinois Press, 1988.

Henderson, Joseph L. "Ancient Myths and Modern Man." *Man and His Symbols.* Edited by Carl G. Jung. Garden City, NY: Doubleday, 1964.

Heuscher, Julius. *A Psychiatric Study of Myths and Fairy Tales: Their Origin, Meaning, and Usefulness.* 2nd ed. Springfield, IL: Thomas, 1974.

International Dictionary of Regional European Ethnology and Folklore. Vol. 1. Copenhagen: Resenkilde and Bagger, 1960.

Ireland, Norma. *Index to Fairy Tales, 1949-1972, Including Folklore, Legends, and Myths, in Collections.* Westwood, MA: F. W. Faxon, 1973.

Jacobs, Joseph. *English Fairy Tales.* Reprint. New York: Dover, 1898.

James, Paula. *Unity in Modernity: A Study of Apuleius' Metamorphoses.* Altertumwissenschaftlichen Texte and Studien. Vol. 16. New York: Olms-Weidman, 1987.

Jason, Heda and Dimitri Segal, eds. *Patterns in Oral Literature.* (World Anthropology). The Hague and Paris: Mouton Publishers, 1977.

Johnson, Edna et al. *Anthology of Children's Literature.* Boston: Houghton Mifflin, 1977.

Jung, C. G. *Man and His Symbols.* New York: Doubleday, 1964.

——— *The Spirit in Man, Art, and Literature.* Translated by R. F. C. Hull. Princeton: Princeton University Press, 1972.

Katz, Phyllis B. "The Myth of Psyche: Definition of the Nature of the Feminine?" *Arethusa* 9, no. 1 (Spring 1976): 111–118.

Kolbenschlag, Madonna. *Kiss Sleeping Beauty Goodbye.* New York: Doubleday, 1979.

Laroque, G. E. "You Gotta Kiss a Lotta Frogs Before You Find Prince Charming." *English Journal* 68(December, 1979): 31-35.

Levi-Strauss, Claude. *Myth and Meaning.* New York: Schocken Books, 1979.

Lewis, C. S. *Of Other Worlds: Essays and Stories.* Edited by Walter Hooper. New York: Harcourt Brace Jovanovich, 1966.

Lieberman, Marcia. "Someday My Prince Will Come: Female Acculturation through the Fairy Tale." *College English* 34 (1972): 383-95.

The Lion and the Unicorn: A Critical Journal of Children's Literature. The Fairy Tale. December, 1988.

Lord, Albert. *The Singer of Tales.* Cambridge, MA: Harvard University Press, 1966.

Lüthi, Max. *The European Folktale: Form and Nature.* Translated by John D. Niles. Bloomington: Indiana University Press, 1982.

———. *The Fairy Tale as Art Form and Portrait of Man.* Bloomington: Indiana University Press, 1984.

———. *Once Upon A Time: On the Nature of Fairy Tales.* New York: Frederick Unger, 1970.

MacDonald, Margaret. *The Storyteller's Sourcebook: A Subject, Title, and Motif Index to Folklore Collections for Children.* Detroit: Neal-Schuman, 1982.

MacPherson, Jay. "'Beauty and the Beast' and Some Relatives." Lecture given to the Friends of the Osbourne and Lillian H. Smith Collections. Toronto, 1974. Mimeo.

Mallet, Carl-Heinz. *Fairy Tales and Children: The Psychology of Children Revealed through Four of Grimm's Fairy Tales.* Translated by Joachim Neugroschel. New York: Schocken Books, 1984.

Meletinsky, Eleazar. "Marriage: Its Function and Position in the Structure of Folktales." In *Soviet Structural Folkloristics.* Vol. 1. Edited by P. Miranda. The Hague and Paris: Mouton, 1974.

Mintz, Thomas. "The Meaning of the Rose in 'Beauty and the Beast.'" *The Psychoanalytic Review* 56, no. 4 (1969–70): 615–20.

Neumann, Erich. *Amor and Psyche: The Psychic Development of the Feminine. A Commentary on the Tale by Apuleius.* Translated from the German by Ralph Manheim. New York: Pantheon, 1956.

O'Suilleabhain, Sean and Reidar Th. Christiansen. *The Types of the Irish Folktale.* Helsinki: Suomalainen Tiedakademia, 1967.

Ong, Walter. *Orality and Literacy.* London: Methuen, 1982.

Ord, Priscilla A., ed. *Proceedings of the Eighth Annual Conference of the Children's Literature Association.* University of Minnesota, March 1981. Boston: Children's Literature Association, 1982.

Pallottino, Paola. "La Bestia Della Bella." *Linea Grafica* (6 November, 1987): 4–13.

Pellowski, Anne. *The World of Storytelling.* New York: Bowker, 1977.

Philip, Neil. "Children's Literature and the Oral Tradition." In *Further Approaches to a Research in*

Children's Literature. Edited by Peter Hunt. 5–22. Proceedings of the Second British Research Seminar in Children's Literature, Cardiff, September 1981. Cardiff: University of Wales, Institute of Science and Technology, Dept. of English, 1982.

Propp, Vladimir. *Morphology of the Folktale.* 2nd ed. Revised and edited by Louis A. Wagner. New introduction by Alan Dundes. Austin: University of Texas Press, 1968.

Radin, Paul. *The Trickster: A Study in American Indian Mythology.* New York: Schocken, 1971.

Raglan, FitzRoy. *The Hero: A Study in Tradition, Myth, and Drama.* New York: Greenwood, 1975 (1956).

Ralston, W. R. S. "Beauty and the Beast." *The Nineteenth Century* (December 1878): 990–1012.

Rowe, Karen. "Feminism and Fairy Tales." *Women's Studies* 6 (1979): 237-57.

Sale, Roger. *Fairy Tales and After: From Snow White to E. B. White.* Cambridge, MA: Harvard University Press, 1978.

Sawyer, Ruth. *The Way of the Storyteller.* Viking, 1942.

Saxby, Maurice, ed. *Through Folklore to Literature.* Sidney: IBBY Australia Publications, 1979. Papers presented at the Australian National Section of the IBBY Conference on Children's Literature, Sydney, 1978.

Schlam, C. C. "The Scholarship on Apulieus since 1938," *Classical World* 64, no. 9 (May 1971): 285–308.

Segel, Elizabeth. "Feminists and Fairy Tales." *School Library Journal* 29, no.5 (January 1983): 30–31.

Shedlock, Marie L. *Art of the Storyteller.* New York: Dover, rev. ed., 1951.

Stahl, Sandra. *Literary Folkloristics and the Personal Narrative.* Bloomington: Indiana University Press, 1989.

Stone, Kay. "Things Walt Disney Never Told Us." In *Women and Folklore.* Edited by Claire R. Farrer. Austin: University of Texas Press, 1975.

Swahn, Jan-Öjvind. *The Tale of Cupid and Psyche.* Lund: Gleerup, 1955.

Tatar, Maria. *The Hard Facts of the Grimms' Fairy Tales.* Princeton: Princeton University Press, 1987.

———. *Off with Their Heads: Fairytales and the Culture of Childhood.* Princeton: Princeton University Press, 1992.

Taylor, Archer. "The Predestined Wife," *Fabula 2* (1959): 45–82.

Thompson, Stith. *The Folktale.* Berkeley: University of California Press, 1977.

———. *Motif-Index of Folk-Literature: A Classification of Narrative Elements in Folktales, Ballads, Myths, Fables, Mediaeval Romances, Exempla, Fabliaux, Jest-books, and Local Legends.* 6 vols. Bloomington: Indiana University Press, 1956.

Toelken, Barre. "The 'Pretty Languages' of Yellowman: Genre, Mode, and Texture in Navaho Coyote Narratives." In *Folklore Genres.* Edited by Dan Ben-Amos. Austin: University of Texas Press, 1983.

Tolkien, J. R. R. "Tree and Leaf." In *The Tolkien Reader.* New York: Ballantine Books, 1966.

Von Franz, Marie-Louise. *A Psychological Interpretation of the Golden Ass of Apuleius.* Irving, TX: Spring Publications, University of Dallas, 1980.

Yolen, Jane. *Touch Magic: Fantasy, Faerie and Folklore in the Literature of Childhood.* New York: Philomel Books, 1981.

Zipes, Jack David. *Breaking the Magic Spell: Radical Theories of Folk and Fairy Tales.* Austin: University of Texas Press, 1979. (Paperback, London: Methuen, 1984).

———. *Fairy Tales and the Art of Subversion: The Classical Genre for Children and the Process of Civilization.* New York: Wildman Press, 1983.

———. "The Origin of the Fairy Tale for Children, or, How Script Was Used To Tame the Beast in Us." In *Children and Their Books: A Celebration of the Work Of Iona and Peter Opie.* Edited by Gillian Avery and Julia Briggs. London: Oxford University Press, 1990.

Ziskind, Sylvia. *Telling Stories to Children.* Wilson, 1976.

Index

by Janet Perlman